D1606763

TRACKS TO THE SEA

NUMBER EIGHTY-THREE
*The Centennial Series of the Association of Former Students,
Texas A&M University*

EARLE B. YOUNG

TRACKS TO
THE SEA

Galveston and Western Railroad Development, 1866–1900

Texas A&M University Press
COLLEGE STATION

**LIBRARY OF CONGRESS
CATALOGING-IN-PUBLICATION DATA**

Young, Earle B., 1929 –
    Tracks to the sea : Galveston and western railroad development,
1866 –1900 / Earle B. Young. — 1st ed.
       p. cm. — (Centennial series of the Association of Former
Students, Texas A&M University ; no. 83)
    Includes bibliographical references and index.
    ISBN 0-89096-883-7 (cloth)
     1. Railroads—Texas—Galveston—History—19th century.
2. Huntington, Collis Potter 1821–1900.   3. Gould, Jay, 1836 –1892.
I. Title. II. Series.
HE2781.G33Y68 1999
385'.09764'139—dc21   98-54146
                                                      CIP

To the memory of John H. Frisby and his wife Margaret.
Frisby, from County Kilkenny, Ireland, arrived in Galveston in 1870
and married Margaret Casey from County Kerry at St. Mary's.

In 1878 Frisby was elected county commissioner and served two terms.
In 1880 he was elected chairman of the Executive Committee of the
Galveston County Democratic Party. He served until 1886.

The Frisbys were my great-grandparents.

CONTENTS

ILLUSTRATIONS

This book was written to stand alone as an account of Galveston's place in the railroad history of the western half of the United States. Nevertheless, it is a companion volume to my first work, *Galveston and the Great West,* the story of harbor improvements—the Deep Water Channel—at Galveston. Both deep water and western railroad connections were necessary for the city to achieve its overriding goal: becoming the seaport for the Great West.

In order to write a story that moves continually forward instead of sideways, I decided to concentrate on only those railroads that were actually completed and played a part in history: the Houston & Great Northern, which later became the International & Great Northern, the Gulf, Colorado & Santa Fe, the Missouri Pacific System, and the Southern Pacific System. The Galveston, Houston & Henderson was completed to Houston before the Civil War and is not included here.

Excluded are sixteen railroads that were proposed, planned, chartered, or partially built between 1866 and 1900. Although these railroads are very interesting individually and as a whole, I have excluded them at this time along with other aspects of Galveston's economic development, such as the cotton trade and manufacturing, for the sake of brevity. Furthermore, the focus of this book is on the part that railroads played in the economic development of Galveston. The emphasis is on corporate strategy and finance rather than organization, construction, and operations.

During the early 1880s, GC&SF president George Sealy was authorized by the board of directors to sell the company on the best terms that he could arrange. This might make it appear that President Sealy was a one-man show. The board members and company officials were very involved, but this book focuses on the activities carried out by the very dynamic president.

Much assistance in the research for this book was provided by the most helpful and knowledgeable staff of the Galveston and Texas History Center at Rosenberg Library in Galveston. Special appreciation is due Connie Menninger, the archivist of the Atchison, Topeka & Santa Fe Railway Collection at the Kansas State Historical Society, Topeka, for assistance with the considerable material there. Her tolerance and cooperation were more than could be expected.

I also extend my appreciation to the staff of the Library of Congress who enabled me to have a very productive visit, those at the Newberry Library in Chicago, and Phyllis E. McLaughlin of Des Moines, who helped me with the Dodge material from the State Historical Society of Iowa.

TRACKS TO THE SEA

When George Sealy, the president of Galveston's Gulf, Colorado & Santa Fe Railway sat down in New York City on August 12, 1885, with railroad tycoons Jay Gould and Collis P. Huntington to agree upon the principles of the Texas Traffic Association (the Texas Pool), a five-year struggle in which Gould attempted to purchase, control, or bankrupt the GC&SF came to an end. The GC&SF's financial posture began to change, making it more attractive to suitors seeking a connection to the Gulf of Mexico. And when the Atchison, Topeka & Santa Fe, Gould's largest rival, acquired the GC&SF in May, 1886, that transaction broke Jay Gould's monopoly on traffic between Texas, Oklahoma, and the Missouri Valley.[1]

This struggle between Gould and Sealy was one of the highlights of the most interesting period of nineteenth-century Texas railroad history, the 1880s. By this time the effects of the Civil War and the terrible depression that followed the Panic of 1873 had worn off and the Industrial Revolution was in full swing. That revolution came to Texas in the form of railroads. By the end of the 1880s, Texas had 8,486 miles of track, 6,046 miles of which was built since 1879. The largest amount of track ever laid in a single year in Texas was 1,527 miles put down in 1881. These events were the beginning of significant economic change in Texas. The railroads were the first large corporations to operate in the state. The rise of these companies was accompanied by tremendous economic and political power, soon followed by the establishment of the Texas Railroad Commission to balance that power. What had heretofore been essentially a rural state began to develop some of the characteristics it would bear in the twentieth century: large, industrialized urban centers and a legislature increasingly beholden to industrial interests.

During this same decade the island city of Galveston, possessing the finest natural harbor on the Texas coast, sought to become the seaport of the states west of the Mississippi River. But this required a deepening of the channels providing access to the inner harbor from the Gulf of Mexico. Sandbars typical of the Texas coast limited access to ships drawing twelve feet or less of water, and twenty-five feet was necessary to handle the ships in planning. The city launched a lobbying effort that eventually resulted in a congressional appropriation enabling the Army Corps of Engineers to provide that deep water channel. After two failed attempts to build jetties into the Gulf of Mexico that would scour a deep water channel between them, Galveston's Deep Water Committee organized a lobbying effort among all of the western states that succeeded in pushing the bill through Congress.

The strategic importance of Galveston evidenced in the 1880s was not entirely new. Texas railroad maps for 1860 and 1870 show Galveston as the focal point for Texas railroads built at that time.[2] It is true that the Galveston, Harrisburg & San Antonio (the GH&SA) and the Houston and Texas Central (the H&TC) converged at Houston, but the city was not a significant port at that time. It was the link to Galveston provided by the Galveston, Houston & Henderson (the GH&H) that made the other roads serving inland Texas feasible. As total Texas trackage reached 9,702 miles by the end of the nineteenth century Galveston's situation remained essentially unchanged.

Maps show that Galveston was the only port with a significant railroad network leading into it. By the end of the century Corpus Christi at Aransas Pass and Beaumont at Sabine Pass were only beginning to reach that point. The existence of railroad connections was one of the main advantages pointed out during the Deep Water Conventions of the 1880s supporting harbor improvements at Galveston. No port could become great without land networks to feed it. Population maps also show that Galveston was closest to the "heart" of Texas. Most of the state's population, its largest cities, and the vast majority of its railroad trackage were in the region to the north of the city. Therefore, it is not surprising that the bulk of Texas imports and exports passed through the port of Galveston. The tracks led to the sea.

This period also saw the entry into Texas of two of the nation's leading railroad tycoons—Gould and Huntington. During this decade Gould took over much of the existing track in Texas, acquiring the Texas & Pacific (T&P), the International & Great Northern, the Missouri, Kansas & Texas (known as the MK&T, or Katy), and the Galveston, Houston & Henderson. Huntington acquired much of the remaining trackage, buying the Houston & Texas Central, the Galveston, Harrisburg & San Antonio, and the Texas & New Orleans. The two also struck a deal between themselves, whereby Huntington's Southern Pacific (SP), building eastward from California, extended his road from El Paso toward San Antonio to meet the GH&SA. Gould, building the T&P westward, met the Southern Pacific at Sierra Blanca in West Texas and used SP trackage to California. Under this arrangement, Gould got his connection to the Pacific but Huntington retained control of the tracks.

The swift attacks by these "railroad generals" soon provided two routes from New Orleans to El Paso with a single route west of there, Gould's being a northern route through Dallas and Fort Worth, Huntington's a southern one by way of Houston and San Antonio. Gould's T&P also had

connections at Dallas with other elements of his Southwestern System
leased to the Missouri Pacific to St. Louis. Huntington eventually acquired connecting lines to his Atlantic port at Newport News, Virginia,
known as the "Huntington System" at that time. In addition three American railroads were building lines in Mexico toward the American border.
Gould saw his Southwestern System extending from St. Louis to Mexico
City, while Huntington was making connections between California and
western Mexico.[3]

These moves across the Texas chessboard by these masters of the game
quickly put Galveston, the state's largest seaport, into a strategic position.
Gould, in the process of building a railroad empire in the Southwest and
Mexico, was interested in augmenting his connections to Mexico with a
steamship line between Galveston and Vera Cruz. Early in the decade he
began making overtures to the Galveston Wharf Company and the business community of the city to provide him terminal facilities for his proposed line of steamers. This plan also required a railroad connection to
Galveston and the purchase, or at least control, of the Gulf, Colorado &
Santa Fe (GC&SF) railroad between Galveston and Fort Worth. Control
of this railroad would save his having to build the Missouri, Kansas &
Texas to the Gulf. Huntington, likewise, had made public his interest in
Galveston for terminal facilities for his Southern Pacific railroad. By the
1880s California had become one of the nation's leading wheat-producing
areas, and the crop needed to be transported to both the Atlantic Coast
of the United States and Europe. Although interested in New Orleans,
Huntington also knew that Galveston presented a shorter haul by railroad
from California. He made known to the Wharf Company and the city
that he would prefer Galveston over New Orleans if the city would deepen
its channel into the Gulf of Mexico enough to allow the largest ships in
use to enter and leave the port.

Gould's and Huntington's interest in Galveston and its railroad provided one of the most intriguing episodes during this dynamic decade, as
Galveston sought to make itself the focal point where railroads from all
over the West met the ships that carried western products to all parts of
the world. Under the dynamic leadership of its president, George Sealy,
the GC&SF was revived from bankruptcy in 1879 and built to Fort Worth
by 1881, followed soon after with a branch to Ballinger in West Texas.
Gould, well-known in the East for his astute but often high-handed
financial and takeover tactics, devoted the first half of the decade to gaining control of the GC&SF, only to have to compromise finally by entering
a pooling arrangement known as the Texas Traffic Association. The survival of this onslaught served to make the GC&SF more attractive to another of Gould's big competitors in the West, and in 1886 the line was sold

to the Atchison, Topeka & Santa Fe (AT&SF) for a sum that was very profitable to its Galveston investors. Sealy's accomplishment in leading the
GC&SF through a successful struggle with the infamous Jay Gould, and
into a merger with the AT&SF, one of the nation's best transcontinental
railroads, certainly put him at the top among nineteenth-century Texas
railroad executives. He may have been the state's most outstanding businessman in any field.

Dallas, Fort Worth, and Houston also became important railroad centers in the vast network of lines crisscrossing the state, but Galveston remained the destination for the state's exports and a point-of-entry for
much of its imports. These cargoes had to move over the two lines leading directly into the city—the GH&H and the GC&SF. Galveston continued to struggle to hold its advantage throughout the nineteenth century.
However, with the coming of Deep Water in 1895, followed by the entry
of the Huntington's Southern Pacific System to its new terminal facilities,
the city ended the century by improving its status as a major port. But, of
course, time never stands still and the competition never sleeps. As the
century wore on, railroad connections between Dallas and St. Louis and
other points east enabled that city to become a great commercial center.
And fifty miles away in Houston, planners were always thinking in terms
of improving that city's direct access to the Gulf of Mexico.

This study focuses on the role that Galveston played in Texas and western railroad history, especially during the 1880s when Gould and Huntington were both involved with the city. This is a study neither of corporate organizational history nor of railroad construction. Instead, it is a
study of corporate strategies and tactics employed by those railroad companies affecting Galveston's economic development. Since the GC&SF of
the 1880s was preceded by GC&SF of the 1870s, which in turn evolved out
of the intensive railroad planning activities immediately after the Civil
War, it will be very helpful to the readers first to review the events of
1865–79 in chapters 1, 2, and 3. The exciting events of the period from
1880 to 1900 are presented in chapters 4 through 8.

As railroad historian Albro Martin has pointed out, "A neglected region in American railroad history continues to be the Southwest."[4] This
study makes use of the secondary sources that have been published but
also places heavy reliance on primary sources that will add new dimen-
sions to previous histories. These sources are particularly useful in presenting the planning activities focused on Galveston during the 1865–72
period; the Gould-Huntington involvement during the 1880s; the secret
negotiations of the Texas Traffic Association agreement between Gould,
Huntington, and Sealy; the sale of the GC&SF; and, finally, the entry of
Huntington's Southern Pacific into Galveston.

PLANNING EFFORTS
FOR NEW RAILROADS

In the first year after the Civil War the people of Texas faced economic dislocations and social changes brought about by four years of war and a peace that ended slavery. Gradually the citizens adjusted to military occupation and began to look to their future, which would be shaped largely by railroads.

The idea for the Houston & Great Northern (H&GN) railroad came from Galveston's railroad planner Caleb G. Forshey. The line was intended as a route to northern Texas along the general route intended for the Galveston, Houston & Henderson (GH&H), which was never built past Houston. The H&GN also led in the 1870s to two major threats to Galveston's very existence. It was a period of change and turmoil, affected by both military occupation and the Panic of 1873. Financing was never easy, and the lack of capital led to takeovers by wealthy New York investors, a trend that continued well past the 1870s as the railroads consolidated into larger and larger organizations.

Willard Richardson's *Galveston Daily News* published an editorial calling attention to a railroad convention to be held at Rusk, Texas, on July 10, 1866, and suggesting that the mayor, city council, chamber of commerce, merchants, and property holders give the matter attention and consider the appointment of delegates. Reminding his readers that it had been eight years since the GH&H from Galveston reached Houston, Richardson pointed out, "The main idea has never been abandoned by intelligent men, that the *road must progress* till middle and northern Texas should be reached. The war has only postponed our enterprises." Displaying the boldness and vision that characterized Richardson in the postwar era, he submitted that the land west of the Mississippi River should be tributary to Galveston and the Gulf of Mexico, and stressed the need for a railroad along the 95th meridian from Galveston and Houston passing near

Huntsville, Rusk, Tyler, and Clarksville, Texas, on to Fort Smith, Arkansas; Council Bluffs, Iowa; and Central Minnesota. He stated:

> A manly effort to secure it will, in a few years, command the unlimited resources and productions, mineral and agricultural, of this vast empire of fertility. Now is the time to project our plans. The more comprehensive, the better. Let the general routes be projected, with such discretion as to accommodate the local and partial enterprises and make them parts of the general plan. By this means our more limited enterprises will have the prestige of great works, and yet will not be cumbered with the necessary completion of the whole. Galveston and Houston should be awake to the conventions, and send their delegates by all means to the Railroad convention at Rusk.[1]

A meeting was held July 3 at the office of Mayor Charles Leonard, who was elected to chair the meeting. After opening remarks by Forshey, a committee, including Albert M. Lea, George B. Nichols, Richardson, and Forshey, was named to draw up resolutions. Richardson may have already prepared the resolutions, based on his editorial of the previous day. Whatever the case, the committee reported its resolutions at the meeting, and they were passed. Boulds Baker, J. C. Smith, John S. Sellers, Dr. J. C. Massie, M. C. McLemore, John S. Sydnor, Dr. William R. Smith (former president of the GH&H), H. B. Andrews, E. B. Settle, and Nichols (superintendent of the GH&H) were selected as members of a delegation. They were instructed to act in conjunction with the delegate appointed by the mayor, Forshey, "whose long experience and familiarity with the topography of the country, and with the most eligible railroad routes, recommended him to the Mayor as a person who would probably be able to present some valuable views to the Convention."[2]

Forshey's involvement with railroad routes began before the Civil War, in 1846, when he published an article in the first volume of the *Commercial Review of the South and West* (later *DeBow's Review*), the leading economic journal in the South at that time, laying out a route for a road from Vidalia, Mississippi, west 101 miles to Bayou Cotile, crossing the Red River at Alexandria, Louisiana.[3] Forshey, who attended the U.S. Military Academy for three years before he began teaching at a college in Mississippi, published another paper in the same journal in 1847, laying out a transcontinental railroad, when various schemes were before Congress seeking funding. Forshey proposed a southern route from Savannah and Charleston to the Pacific at Mazatlan, Mexico, pointing out that his route was 900 miles shorter just from the Mississippi to the Pacific than one of the other proposals. He also presented this idea at the Memphis Commercial Convention in November, 1845.[4]

When Forshey first moved to Galveston in 1855 to found the Texas Military Academy, he no doubt quickly became aware of the railroad planning activities taking place in Galveston and Texas. A convention had been held on July 15, 1852, to address the requirements of the rapidly growing state. It concluded by proposing a State Internal Improvement Fund as a source of railroad financing and sought an extra session of the Texas Legislature to consider the proposal. The chairman of the committee to write the report was Galveston lawyer Lorenzo Sherwood. He played a leading role in the convention, perhaps even shaping the final report, but Governor P. H. Bell failed to act on the recommendation.[5]

When Forshey arrived in Galveston, Sherwood had gained attention for his State Plan, a system of state-financed and owned railroad. His ideas had been set forth in some detail in three articles in *DeBow's Review* in 1855. Forshey also set forth a plan in *DeBow's* defining routes and a financing system. His routes were somewhat similar to the 1852 report, which had a main line to the Red River from Galveston, with branches going east and west. Forshey called for a trunk line between Galveston and Houston, with four branches in the directions of Fulton, Arkansas (northeast); Grayson County, between the Trinity and Brazos Rivers (north); Austin (northwest); and San Antonio (west). Forshey did not accept Sherwood's state financing plan. Instead he proposed that the state furnish materials and private corporations provide roadbeds and superstructure. He also disagreed with Sherwood that the state should provide roads to communities, even forcing them if the community was unwilling to help in the construction.[6]

Neither Sherwood's State Plan nor the modifications offered by Forshey or Richardson met any success in prewar Texas. The Corporate Plan—private financing assisted by state land grants or loans from the permanent school fund—won the day. However, when the citizens of Texas were ready to start railroad planning following the war, Forshey was ready to return to the wars. The Rusk Convention would have provided the first opportunity, but unfortunately he missed the train. Nevertheless, for the benefit of his fellow Texans (and future historians) he spelled out his ideas in two lengthy articles published in the *Daily News*. In fact, McLemore was the only named delegate who actually went. He reported a great deal of earnestness in the support for railroad construction with general agreement upon state land grants and taxation in counties along the routes as the means of attracting private financing.[7]

The route that Forshey proposed in his article was essentially the same road up the 95th meridian that Richardson had suggested in his July editorial, and an extension of the route through northeast Texas that Forshey had proposed in his 1855 article in *DeBow's Review*. Forshey elaborated on the fertility, minerals, and other wealth of the sixteen counties in Northeast Texas that would have access to his road. He also pointed out that the route from Arkansas to New Orleans through Shreveport was five hundred miles longer than the distance to Galveston, a positive factor in directing the trade of this area to Galveston. Unlike the people of East Texas, he emphasized the importance of building railroads as part of systems, or networks, instead of point to point. The "system" he envisioned for this road included the three railroads already under construction from Houston: the Buffalo Bayou, Brazos & Colorado to the west; the Houston & Texas Central to the north; and the Texas & New Orleans to the east. In North Texas he envisioned his road intersecting with the transcontinental roads proposed to the Pacific Ocean, perhaps even sharing sections of track with them when possible. The trunk road between Galveston and Houston would grow to three or four tracks to handle the connections at Houston. The name he suggested for this line up the 95th meridian was the Houston & Great Northern.[8]

An article by Albert M. Lea appeared immediately after Forshey's, pointing out the advantages of a supplementary road from Galveston to the Pacific Ocean at Mazatlan, Mexico, along the lines that Forshey had advocated in his article in *DeBow's* almost twenty years earlier.[9] Galveston was fortunate to have these two West Point-trained engineers at this critical point in the city's history. This was not, however, their first appearance on the island. Both, as Confederate Army Engineers, had participated in the Battle of Galveston and earned General John Bankhead Magruder's commendation for their roles, and General Magruder recommended Lea for promotion for his performance.[10]

Lea graduated from West Point in 1831. He remained in the Army for five years, after which he held a number of civil engineering positions. He was the city engineer at Knoxville when he accepted a position as the chief engineer of the Aransas Railroad Company and moved to Texas. At this time Forshey was the chief engineer of the GH&H. Forshey had attended West Point from 1833 until 1836, where he was classmate of future Generals Braxton Bragg, Jubal Early, and Joseph Hooker. He left West Point after three years to teach engineering at Jefferson College in Washington, Mississippi. Before coming to Galveston, he worked for the Corps of Engineers at Vidalia, Louisiana, studying the hydrology of the Mississippi River and the geology of the Mississippi Delta. Both Forshey and Lea were probably well known in Galveston. Lea's tragedy at the Battle of Galveston most certainly brought him the sympathy of all Galveston residents.

In a very moving passage, Charles W. Hayes described how Major Lea arrived after the battle at the Union ship *Harriet Lane* to find his son, Lieutenant-Commander Edward Lea, executive office of the ship, lying mortally wounded on the deck. Young Lea died in the arms of his father, who also read the services the next day at his burial.[11]

As an outgrowth of the Rusk Convention, another invitation went out for a follow-up meeting at Tyler to be held on September 11, 1866. The letter stated a need for action but did not set a specific agenda. Later information attributed to the *Palestine News* indicated one of the prime objects of the gathering would be to address the feasibility of a road from Navasota, on the Houston & Texas Central Railroad, through Palestine and Tyler to Clarksville to connect with another road under discussion to come south from Missouri. In preparation for the meeting, the Galveston Chamber of Commerce held a meeting where both Lea and Forshey presented their ideas on railroads. Charles R. Hughes, who presided, named a committee of A. C. McKeen, Thomas H. McMahan, and J. M. Swisher to select a delegation. Initially, those chosen were Dr. William R. Smith, Mayor Charles H. Leonard, Hughes, Forshey, and Lea, but Forshey and Lea withdrew and were replaced by John Sealy and L. M. Hitchcock.[12]

The Tyler meeting resulted in a memorial to the Texas Legislature requesting that state aid be limited to major roads benefiting the whole state. It recommended as main roads the Southern Pacific (the forerunner of the Texas & Pacific) operating between Marshall and Shreveport, and a road north from Galveston, essentially along the 95th meridian, serving the large area between the Sabine and Trinity Rivers. Although this obviously was Forshey's H&GN, the specifics of the route were left open, perhaps as a compromise between the Marshall and Tyler interests who were both vying to run the line through their respective cities. The resolution was signed by Richard B. Hubbard, F. M. Hays, and James M. Douglas. The legislature, while not yet addressing the matter of state aid, acted quickly on the charter for the H&GN. The third reading was held on October 18, 1866, and passed on October 22. Among those named as applicants on the charter were E. B. Nichols of Galveston and William J. Hutchins, H. D. Taylor, William Marsh Rice, and B. A. Shepherd, all of Houston. Moses Taylor, president of the First National Bank of New York, was known to be a backer of the road.[13]

The charter for the Central Transit Company, the route proposed by Albert Lea running from Galveston to Mazatlan on the Pacific Ocean, was approved November 6, 1866. Pryor Lea, the promoter, came to Goliad in 1846 and became interested in railroads in the Aransas Pass area. He was involved with the Aransas Railroad Company, which had hired Albert M. Lea as its chief engineer. That road, chartered to operate between Aransas Pass and Goliad, changed its name to the Central Transit before the Civil War. Pryor Lea apparently obtained a new charter under the same name for a new road traversing a greater distance. At the same time that the Central Transit was announced, Albert M. Lea claimed that as a result of his influence that road had changed its terminus from Aransas Pass to Galveston where it could connect with roads from the north and east. The charter provided that at least seven of the incorporators must have their first meeting at Washington, D.C., in January, 1867, and obtain subscriptions of one million dollars and reorganization by the stockholders within two years.[14]

THE HOUSTON & GREAT NORTHERN RAILROAD

While nothing was heard from the Central Transit immediately, the H&GN quickly went about the process of raising subscriptions for its stock. The *Rusk Observer* carried an appeal to the citizens of East Texas published by a committee headed by Dr. C. G. Young, president of the Chappell Hill Manufacturing Company and general superintendent of the company's ironworks near Rusk. The committee's appeal identified a number of economic advantages that would accrue to the citizens of East Texas if the road were built. A savings of $320 for every 20 bales of cotton could be realized on the cost of moving the cotton to market. The road could be expected in ten years to increase by $10,000 the wealth of every farmer on its route who had 400 acres of land, with 75 acres in cultivation and making 20 bales of cotton. The availability of transportation would cause the iron mines of East Texas to be opened, and cotton and woolen factories, sawmills, and flouring mills to spring up along its line. The appeal also pointed out the mutual advantage to both Galveston and the interior country of a great railroad connected with a great seaport. As an initial financing plan, the committee recommended that each county along the line subscribe $10,000, that private subscriptions in Galveston and Houston be made for $300,000, and that the two cities, that is, city governments, raise $1,500,000 each by issuing bonds.[15]

By June 1, 1867, the H&GN had organized, electing Dr. Young president: E. C. Stockton secretary; and Peter J. Willis, who had recently moved to Galveston from Houston, treasurer. No sooner had the H&GN organized than Dr. Young began the drive for stock subscriptions in Galveston. Not surprisingly, Willard Richardson, who almost a year earlier had made a railroad along the 95th meridian a public issue, strongly supported the subscription drive in the columns of the *Galveston Daily News*.

He pointed out the impact that railroads had in the development of Boston, New York, Chicago, and New Orleans, and how the railroads were often the key to survival and growth. He also pointed out Galveston's dependence upon a single crop, cotton, and how Galveston's business failed when the cotton crop failed. The H&GN would expand the city's economic base by reaching into the wheat country, challenging Chicago, and would benefit the city's foundries and machine shops with the supply of pig iron from Cherokee and Anderson Counties. Richardson proposed a goal of $100,000 in private subscriptions, a much more modest target than the $300,000 suggested by Dr. Young. He proposed that the largest business houses take $10,000 each, the largest landholders and other businesses take $5,000, with the smallest taking $1,000 to $500. Finally, he pointed out that Houston and the counties along the route had made their initial subscriptions; Galveston was now on the spot and others were watching.[16]

A group of Galveston businesses called a public meeting on Saturday, June 15, 1867, to open the stock sale. In a separate article accompanying the announcement, the *Daily News* reported that Dr. Young had raised $40,000 in Houston in the previous week and said that Galveston should raise $250,000, doubling the earlier goal. The Strand Street merchants should raise $100,000, with the rest coming from property holders and other merchants and businesses. "The time has come for Galveston to show her hand and do something, and the man or men who have the ability, and yet will draw in their heads like turtles . . . will be marked, as they ought to be, and pronounced sordid and selfish," the newspaper proclaimed.[17]

At the meeting Richardson was elected chairman, and T. F. White was chosen secretary. Dr. Young addressed the meeting, after which a resolutions committee, composed of Allen Lewis, T. F. White, and Forshey, presented a resolution expressing support of the H&GN and requesting the county to subscribe to $1,000,000 in stock. A committee consisting of Cyrus Thompson, J. C. Smith, Marcus F. Mott, M. C. McLemore, and Lewis was chosen to assist Dr. Young in canvassing for the subscriptions. Leading citizens of San Antonio were introduced at the meeting and presented a proposed road from Columbus to San Antonio. This road would connect with the Buffalo Bayou, Brazos & Colorado at Columbus, thus providing Galveston with a through route to San Antonio. Those attending the meeting also passed a resolution asking the county to subscribe to $300,000 of this road's stock, and naming A. Neill, T. Mather, and R. M. Tevis to the subscription committee.[18]

The June 15 meeting was adjourned, to be resumed on June 18. Then reality began to set in. The military governor of Texas, General Charles

Griffin, informed the San Antonians that there was not any legal state government or laws properly in force. He also stated told that no elections would be held by counties or cities to authorize such subscriptions. Mc-Mahan addressed the meeting and said that, as much as he felt voluntary subscriptions were an unfair method of financing railroads, he would favor that approach over doing nothing. He was followed by Dr. Young, a man of great enthusiasm as well as ability, who reviewed all of the positive factors—the vast resources, wealth, population, and products of the rich counties of the state through which the road would pass; the immense amount of trade that would be diverted to Galveston and away from Shreveport and New Orleans; and the financial and material benefits that would accrue over the years to Galveston. He stated that if he could get just $300,000 from all sources, he could grade the first fifty miles. Then, if in a year the counties could be authorized to make subscriptions, he could pay for the iron and lay the first fifty miles of track. Step by step, with private subscriptions, he knew the road could be built.[19]

But more than enthusiasm is required to build railroads, and circumstances conspired against Dr. Young and his supporters. The uncertainties of military government and the coming Reconstruction, and the lack of capital because of the lagging economic conditions, worked to prevent any progress on the H&GN from occurring before 1870. Another factor that may have affected the H&GN was the condition of the GH&H at this time. After all, that line was the connection to the H&GN at Houston. The GH&H had just been placed under receiver Tipton Walker by the court as a result of the suit by N. A. Cowdrey against the current owners. Those individuals named in the suit—George B. Nichols, J. L. Briggs, L. M. Hitchcock, Ebenezer B. Nichols, John H. Hutchings, William R. Smith, Robert Mills, E. S. Wood, John Sealy, Thomas H. McMahan, S. Southwick, George Ball, and J. W. Jockusch—must have faced additional uncertainty that may have discouraged their participation in any new railroad adventures in 1867. It is noteworthy that the partners of Ball, Hutchings Company, the city's and perhaps the state's largest bank—George Ball, John Sealy, and John H. Hutchings—were conspicuously absent from the activities surrounding the H&GN. If they failed to subscribe to stock, it may have had a negative influence on other members of the business community.

FORSHEY SUPPORTS THE INTERNATIONAL

In a published letter to the president of the Galveston Chamber of Commerce regarding an upcoming meeting of the National Board of

Trade, Forshey put forth his suggestions on two issues for which board support should be sought. The first was the need for action by the federal government to prevent the inner bar from closing off Galveston from the Gulf of Mexico. The second suggestion was to support the railroad route recently proposed, the International, that would connect Cairo, Illinois, and the Mississippi River with Mazatlan, Mexico, via Little Rock, Arkansas, and San Antonio, Texas. He felt that this route, 1,450 miles in length, was more practical and economical than the other route under consideration from St. Louis to San Diego, a distance of 1,800 miles. Furthermore, with a slight defection to the south the International route could connect with the existing roads in Texas, connecting Galveston with the Pacific, 925 miles away.[20]

In a follow-up article the next month, Forshey again summarized his views on "The Two Great Railroad Enterprises." He repeated from his earlier article the arguments for the trunk line north from Galveston along the 95th meridian, through Tyler to Kansas. He also referred to an article in *DeBow's Review* that described it as "the greatest undeveloped railroad enterprise on earth." The second great enterprise was the International to Mazatlan. Here he reminded the readers of his participation in the Memphis Commercial Conventions of 1845 and 1849, and of his article in *DeBow's* in 1847 advocating the short route to the Pacific. Forshey repeated his description of the route offered twenty-two years before. However, this time he addressed the matter of the route across Mexico, admitting that the Cordillera Mountains in the State of Durango would present many obstacles for 100 miles or more. Nevertheless, he said, the precious metals in those mountains would make the additional expenses economical.[21]

In December Forshey reported to the Galveston Chamber of Commerce that arrangements had been made to insure the construction of the H&GN, and he spoke enthusiastically of interest of the citizens of Kansas and Missouri to connect with the Texas road. Forshey represented Galveston at the Commercial Convention at Louisville where he made presentations on the need for Harbor Improvement at Galveston as well as on Galveston's support for a Pacific railroad over the southern route. Later, at the Cincinnati Convention, Forshey would make the report for the Committee on Trans-latitudinal Railroads, in which he recommended six north-south routes, including the one from St. Paul to Galveston. He specifically recommended the H&GN and the International for congressional aid. Through Forshey's participation in the Southern Commercial Conventions and the meetings of the National Board of Trade, Galveston was beginning to take its place on the agenda of needed internal improvements.[22]

The arrangements Forshey referred to in his report to the chamber of commerce were explained in December, 1869, by Dr. Young, president of the H&GN, in a letter to stockholders and supporters of the road. Forshey, as agent of the H&GN, had negotiated a conditional contract with James F. Joy of Detroit, a well-known railroad executive, to build the line once all obstacles and conditions were met. Passage through the Indian Territory, now the state of Oklahoma, was the first problem. Negotiations were under way to acquire rights, but, Young said, congressional action might be necessary. He also outlined the financing method, based upon land donations and stock subscriptions by landowners on the route and contributions from counties on the line.[23]

Dr. Young urged quick action by all those involved in the plans, "that they may reap the benefits of the powerful capitalists and railroad organizations with which this conditional contract has been effected." Joy, who was associated with Boston capitalists John Murray Forbes, Nathaniel Thayer, Moses Taylor, and others, had been involved with the development of Michigan railroads before the Civil War. He became president of the Michigan Central and led that road's expansion into Chicago. As a result of legal battles there, he hired a young lawyer named Abraham Lincoln to work for him. Later Joy became president of the Chicago, Burlington & Quincy as he moved westward. Then he broke ranks with the Forbes group and began acquiring his own empire in Missouri and Kansas, acquiring the Hannibal & St. Joseph, the Kansas & Neosho Valley (renamed the Missouri River, Fort Scott & Gulf), and the Leavenworth, Lawrence & Galveston (LL&G).[24]

By the time Joy made this move, and Dr. Young had Forshey contract with Joy to build the H&GN, the Kansas roads being built south to the Indian Territory had been attracting attention in Galveston for two years. In January, 1868, the *Galveston Daily News* called attention to the progress of the LL&G, known in Kansas as "the Galveston road," which had completed its first thirty miles. The potential connections with all of the western area of the nation were pointed out, and the future prospects for Galveston as the seaport to this region were hailed. The future of Galveston as described in that *Daily News* editorial of May, 1866, advocating the city as the seaport of the Great West was beginning to take shape. When the Missouri River, Fort Scott & Gulf Railroad was authorized by Congress to cross the Indian Territory, the company announced its plan to connect at the Red River with the H&TC. Richardson visited Chicago in September, 1869, following Joy's acquisition of both the LL&G and the Fort Scott lines, and provided his Galveston readers with a lengthy report on the state of railroad building in the Midwest and Kansas in particular.

At that time he described the company, popularly known as the Joy roads, as owning the Michigan Central, the Chicago, Burlington & Quincy, four other roads in the Iowa-Nebraska-Kansas-Missouri area, as well as the Fort Scott and the LL&G. Richardson reported that the two roads under construction toward the Indian Territory—the Fort Scott and the LL&G—would probably strike the border about 50 miles apart, then unite about halfway across the Indian Territory and reach the Texas border as a single trunk line. Richardson indicated they would connect there with the H&TC within three years.[25]

At the beginning of 1870 Galveston was faced with the happy prospect, on paper at least, of two railroads connecting the seaport with Kansas City and points north and west—the H&TC/Joy road combination, and the H&GN, which would have to seek a new connection. At this time the H&TC had passed Hearne and was approaching Bremond, both new towns built as the railroad arrived. Unfortunately, we have no explanation for Joy's planning to construct the H&GN while at the same time intending to connect with the H&TC. Nevertheless, in March the H&GN was moving right ahead with its plans. First, the president and the executive committee were authorized by the board of directors to take the necessary steps to have the road surveyed and built from Houston to the Trinity River in the shortest possible time. It was suggested that the decision to act was related to the naming of two new directors, E. H. Cushing and Benjamin A. Botts, both of Houston, to the board, replacing S. L. Hoenthal and T. R. Bonner. On March 22, the H&GN announced that one of the country's most experienced railroad engineers, C. E. Noble, had arrived from New York to take charge of construction and that Dr. Young was on his way back from New York where he made arrangements for the work to proceed immediately.[26]

The arrangements made in New York were later fully explained in another letter from Dr. Young to the stockholders and interested citizens. First he announced that a group of New York investors had purchased the entire $6,000,000 capital stock of the company, except for the $100,000 subscribed before the company was organized. The group was headed by William Earl Dodge and Walter Phelps, who had been reported visiting in the South a year earlier. Others identified were Moses Taylor, John I. Blair, and Joseph H. Scranton. Dr. Young said of them, "No men in America stand any higher than the gentlemen whose names I have mentioned and their associates." With $295,000 paid in cash, he said that construction could get under way immediately and proceed as fast as possible. But, he added, he made certain representations to the investors to secure their support that would require the compliance of those affected. First, their investment would be protected by the laws of the state. Second, the right of way for the road would be freely granted by the owners of the land. Third, landowners contiguous to the line would make generous land donations, conditioned by the rapid progress of construction. Fourth, state aid would be requested only if it was received by other roads.[27]

This very positive development with the H&GN was quickly followed by equally encouraging events with the Joy roads. General W. T. Clarke, Galveston's representative in Congress, introduced a bill to incorporate the Kansas, Indian Territory & Gulf Railway Company and to enable the Fort Scott and LL&G roads to unite and construct a single track through the Indian Territory to the Gulf. However, Joy's plans encountered an obstacle when the Union Pacific (Southern Branch), soon to be known as the Missouri, Kansas & Texas (the Katy), challenged Joy's right to cross the Indian Territory.[28]

While Richardson and his newspaper had been paying attention to the plans and progress of Joy roads for the past eighteen months, the Katy had built quietly and rapidly southward from Fort Riley, reaching the border of the Indian Territory at Humboldt on June 6, 1870, ahead of both Joy roads. Timing was not the factor, however, in determining who had the right to cross the Indian Territory. Katy General Manager Robert S. Stevens maintained that under the act of Congress the road had to follow the Neosho River Valley, where Humboldt was located. Baxter Springs, where the Fort Scott line had reached the Indian Territory, was not in the Valley. Stevens appealed to Secretary of the Interior Jacob D. Cox, who recommended the Katy to President Grant, who approved. Thus suddenly it was the Katy that now would be building to the Gulf, announcing its intention "to celebrate our Fourth of July, two years hence in Galveston."[29]

THREATS TO GALVESTON'S POSITION

With the Joy roads now completely out of the picture and the Katy firmly planning to meet the Houston & Texas Central at Denison near the Texas border, it was necessary for Dr. Young and the board of directors to alter their plans for the H&GN. The first indication of change came quickly. After increasing their stock holdings in three railroads running out of Houston, plus the International, which was chartered in 1870 and planning to build from Hearne to Longview, the New York investors were ready to make their move.

When the directors and officers of the H&GN were announced after the meeting of the stockholders in December, 1870, New Yorkers Moses Taylor, William Earl Dodge, and William Walter Phelps joined the board along with the familiar Houston names, William Marsh Rice, William J. Hutchins, and Cornelius Ennis. Phelps was elected vice president to President C. G. Young. The annual meeting of the H&TC on May 6, 1872, marked the entry of the Dodge-Phelps interests into that railroad's control. The directors elected at this meeting included Moses Taylor and Dodge from New York along with the Houstonians who had been managing the company, William Marsh Rice, William J. Hutchins, Paul Bremond, Abram Groesbeeck, Cornelius Ennis, W. R. Baker, A. J. Burke, and T. M. Shirley. Thomas A. Peirce, who had recently taken over the Galveston, Harrisburg & San Antonio (formerly the Buffalo Bayou, Brazos & Colorado) as well as the GH&H, was also named a director.[30]

In March, 1872, plans for a great port at the mouth of the Brazos River were announced by the combined interests of four railroads—the Houston & Great Northern, the Houston & Texas Central, the International, and the Houston Tap & Brazoria. By this time Dodge was president of the H&TC, and Galusha Grow had replaced Dr. Young as president of the H&GN. Large purchases of land had been made in the area surrounding the mouth of the Brazos, and real estate speculation was as much a part of the scheme as creating a land-sea transportation network. The threat to Galveston was obvious and immediate since studies made by the Dodge-Phelps interests indicated that for a comparatively small expense a harbor with 18 feet of water at the entrance could be developed, whereas Galveston had but 10 feet. A rival port could potentially eclipse a city like Galveston, not yet a great city, whereas New Orleans, Savannah, or Charleston with their large capital investments would be immune. The *Railroad Gazette* noted the increasing tendency of railroads to invest in land with the purpose of having land values increase to offset the losses in the early years of railroad operation. Duluth and San Diego were cited as examples of such port developments.[31]

Another outside player, Charles Morgan, was also looming on the horizon at this time. Hardly an "outsider," since he had been operating ships between New Orleans and the Texas ports since the 1840s, Morgan entered the Texas railroad scene when he acquired the San Antonio & Mexican Gulf Railroad Company and the Indianola Railroad Company, and merged them into the Gulf, Western Texas & Pacific Railway Company, a move approved by the Texas Legislature on May 19, 1871. In December, 1871, he merged the New Orleans, Mobile & Texas Railroad with his Opelousas road, thus acquiring the franchise of the Texas & New Orleans, the line building east from Houston to the Sabine River. In other words, Morgan had now rapidly expanded his land-sea empire to the extent that he could connect San Antonio to New Orleans by land and sea routes, both going around Galveston. This eventuality prompted a young

lawyer with a bright future in front of him, Thomas P. Ochiltree, to propose that Galveston offer Morgan a subsidy of $500,000 to bring his
Texas-bound line from Beaumont to Galveston instead of Houston.[32]

Ochiltree said that earlier in the year during the Central Transit vote
he had been authorized by the New Orleans & Mobile road, also known
as the Chattanooga, to make such a request of Galveston. He could not
speak for Morgan, but he thought that the idea would still have appeal.
However, it is doubtful that Morgan would have been interested in 1872.
His relations with Galveston were already beginning to sour as a result of
the close working arrangements the Galveston Wharf Company was
making with Morgan's competitor, the Mallory line, and also as a result of
Galveston's frequent quarantines of New Orleans, which worked to favor
the Mallory line and New York merchants.[33]

At the same time to the North events of major importance to all of the
railroad players in Texas were occurring. In his annual report of May 4,
1872, Milton G. Howe, chief engineer of the H&TC, stated that the line's
route had been completed to a point 25 miles north of Corsicana, another
30 miles to Dallas had been graded, and engineering parties were in the
field locating the line from Dallas to the Red River near Sherman. By early
1873 the H&TC reached Denison and the Katy, which had built south
across the Indian Territory. The Katy probably became of interest to
Texas railroad interests when the Kansas Legislature approved a charter
on April 4, 1870, that included plans for building across Texas via Waco
and Austin to the Rio Grande River and Mexico. The Texas Legislature
approved these plans, passing a resolution on August 2, 1870. While not a
charter, the resolution granted the Katy the same rights and privileges as
a company chartered in Texas. The resolution included some tax exemp-
tions and protective clauses against state-subsidized competition.

With the dynamic leadership provided by President Levi Parsons and
General Manager Robert S. Stevens and the financial support of wealthy
New Yorkers such as August Belmont, J. Pierpont Morgan, Levi P. Mor-
ton, and a young Cleveland oil man named John D. Rockefeller, the Katy
built steadily south across the Indian Territory to its rendezvous with
the H&TC at Denison. The actual physical interchange of track was
completed on March 18, 1873, and it would not be long before the connecting companies were claiming run times of 92.5 hours, Galveston to New
York; 90 hours, Houston to New York; 52.1 hours, Galveston to St. Louis;
and 49.5 hours, Houston to St. Louis. Obviously, the importance of this
event for all Texas railroad and commercial interests was enormous.
Whereas all previous railroad developments had connected the interior of
the state with the Gulf of Mexico, this new line also connected the inte-

rior of Texas with growing commercial centers such as Kansas City and St. Louis and threatened to totally disrupt trading patterns that had been in existence since the early settling of Texas.[34]

MORGAN TAKES OVER THE H&TC

In 1873 the H&GN and the International were merged into the I&GN, including the Houston Tap & Brazoria. All of these roads were now under the control of Dodge, Phelps, and Taylor. Although news of the development of a new port at the mouth of the Brazos River persisted, the GH&H, now also controlled by northern capitalists, continued to connect both the I&GN and the H&TC to Galveston. However, subsequent events made it very clear that the Dodge-Phelps combine was out to change the railroad map of Texas. According to historian George C. Werner, the H&TC built its track from Corsicana to Red River City at what is now standard width (4 feet, 8$\frac{1}{2}$ inches), causing a break with the earlier track to the south built to the state-required 5 feet, 8$\frac{1}{2}$ inches. In 1875 the H&TC changed its tracks from Corsicana south to Hearne, leaving only the 120 miles between Hearne and Houston at the wider gauge. After Herbert M. Hoxie became manager at the GH&H, the decision was made to convert the remaining 120 miles of the H&TC and the 50 miles of the GH&H to smaller gauge—all in one day. The railroad made plans, ordered and put in place materials, and organized work crews. On July 29, 1876, with Hoxie directing the work on the GH&H and chief engineer Milton G. Howe in charge on the H&TC, the entire 170 miles was changed, providing direct connections with the MKT and St. Louis without the previously required transfers because of different track widths.[35]

The I&GN held great interest for Galveston also, especially after stories began circulating about plans for the new port at Velasco, the mouth of the Brazos River. The merger of the International and the H&GN at once seemed to dovetail into those plans. The merger was put into effect in December, 1872, when Hoxie was made general manager of both lines, even though the approval of the legislature was not obtained until March, 1875. At this time the H&GN extended from Houston north to Palestine, 150 miles, and the I&GN built 177 miles from Longview to Hearne. In this configuration, the International connected with the H&TC at Hearne, the former H&GN at Palestine, and the Texas & Pacific at Longview, providing two routes out of the states to the north and east for the Dodge-Phelps lines.[36]

Thoughts of Velasco and other worries were probably on the minds of Galveston businessmen when Dodge and Phelps, along with a party of wealthy easterners, visited Galveston on March 3, 1877, while on a tour of Texas. Included in the group were John I. Blair, president of three railroads and director of fourteen others, including the H&TC and the I&GN; Thomas W. Pearsall, director of the I&GN; Samuel Thorne of New York, president of the Duchess & Columbia Railroad; Galusha Grow, ex-president of the I&GN and former Speaker of the House of Representatives; C. J. Nourse of Pennsylvania; N. S. Easton of New York; and William Dodge Stokes, also a member of the Phelps, Dodge & Company mining and railroad empire. They were also accompanied by Abram Groesbeeck, vice president of the H&TC; Robert S. Hayes, vice president of the I&GN; and General Superintendent Hoxie. The group arrived in Houston via the H&TC, examined facilities there, and then moved to Morgan's port at Clinton, where they took the steamer *Diana* to Galveston. They arrived in Galveston late Saturday and spent Sunday touring the city and its attractions, then left on Monday. The *New York Times* stated that "the special object of the party is to familiarize themselves with the railroads of Texas with a view to determining further business movements and investments, and to inform Northern capitalists interested in them how the railroad system of Texas works and of the general condition of the roads in which they are specially interested."[37]

Later in the month Hayes and Hoxie brought another group of eastern and European financiers to Galveston while on a tour of Texas and the H&TC and I&GN railroads. This party included Theodore Roosevelt of New York, director of the Bank of Commerce and the father of a future president; Robert Winthrop of New York, banker and capitalist; J. S. Kennedy of New York, banker and former president of the I&GN; Staunton Blake of Boston, of the banking firm of Blake Bros. of Boston, London, and Edinburgh; William John Menzies, managing director of the Scottish-American Investment Company; and T. Houstoun-Boswell, son of Sir George Houstoun-Boswell, Baronet of Blackadder, Scotland. No one revealed specific purposes for the visit, but it appears that the Dodge-Phelps empire envisioned expansion, with or without the port at Velasco.[38]

One would have thought that the Dodge-Phelps empire was faltering when the H&TC was sold to the Morgan interests on March 24, 1877, shortly after the Galveston visit, and the I&GN went into receivership on April 1, 1878. This was not to be the end of their involvement in Texas, however. On August 1, 1879, the bondholders of the I&GN purchased the road for $1,000,000. George Sealy represented the trustees for the bondholders, Kennedy and Sloan of New York, and reported that the sale would relieve the bondholders, who were also the principal stockholders, of the complications involved in the receivership. Sealy indicated that the current management would probably stay the same and the company would probably begin a new construction program.[39]

The Dodge-Phelps plans for the Brazos were not dead either; they became an issue in the 1878 election for the congressional district containing Galveston. According to a dispatch from Austin to the *Daily News*, Dodge, Phelps, and the other "money kings of Wall Street" who had conceived the idea of building a great commercial and manufacturing city at the mouth of the Brazos were supporting Congressman George W. (Wash) Jones, who ironically was a Greenback opposed to Wall Street. It was understood that Jones would push for government financing to remove the bar at the mouth of the river and to build a navy shipyard at the site. To achieve this goal the Dodge-Phelps interests had already purchased the Houston Tap & Brazoria railroad and several thousand acres of land in the area. As evidence of Galveston's concern over Jones's candidacy, the correspondent pointed out that the county delegation to the convention at Brenham had included Judge William P. Ballinger, who had earlier turned down the nomination for governor, and other strong personages.[40] In reference to Ballinger, the reporter said: "Why was he found upon such an errand, ostensibly playing second fiddle in such a delegation, if down underneath all this did not linger some matter of vital importance to his city?"[41] Whether the Wall Street support of Wash Jones was political gossip or fact, it was true at the time that the Dodge-Phelps plans were progressing and were a matter of concern.

Financial difficulties, however, continued to plague the Dodge-Phelps combine. A group of unnamed creditors filed legal proceedings on March 19, 1877, to have a receiver named. While embarrassing to the management, the problem, it was pointed out, was that of a railroad that could currently be built for $15,000 per mile staggering under the combined load of operating expenses, dividends to stockholders, and interest contracted on debt when building costs were $30,000 per mile. In other words, the H&TC was another victim of the Panic of 1873 and the depressed conditions that followed the earlier inflated conditions when the road was built. There was a bright spot in the dark clouds as far as Galveston was concerned, however. Since the same creditors controlled the H&TC and the I&GN, it was conceivable that Galveston could be made the terminus of the two roads instead of Houston or Velasco. Galusha Grow, when president of the I&GN, had favored Galveston as a terminus, and now it was rumored that he might become the receiver. On the following day, March 10, 1877, in hearings at Austin, Dodge, president of the H&TC, was charged with acting in collusion with Phelps, representing the creditors, in a move to deprive the original Texas owners of their interest in the company. It also came out that the company owed the Texas School Fund $600,000 and owed the state $80,000 in taxes. At this point Charles Morgan entered the picture in the role of a friend of the Houston shareholders who might relieve them of both their debt and their railroad, or at least their share of it, in return for his beneficence.[42]

The plight of the H&TC played right into the hands of Morgan and his desire for control of interior connections to his port at Clinton. The sale of the H&TC to the Morgan interests on March 24, 1877, must not have come as a surprise to many, especially the businessmen of Galveston. With Morgan now in control of the H&TC, the future of Galveston was as much in jeopardy as it would be from a new port at Velasco. The H&TC board of directors passed resolutions nullifying Dodge's action in accepting service of the suit and declared his actions nonbinding on the company. It was also declared that Morgan would pay all debts due or that thereafter might become due, and that he may receive all bonds and hold them with the same rights as the original bondholders. He met the April interest and tax payments of the road, purchased 40,440$^{1}/_{2}$ shares of the HT&C in the market, and acquired proxies for 7,035 shares from John J. Cisco and 6,675$^{1}/_{2}$ shares from Dodge. At the May 7, 1877, stockholders meeting, Morgan purged the board of the Dodge-Phelps-Taylor group, and the stockholders elected as directors Morgan, Charles A. Whitney, Alexander C. Hutchinson, and Charles Fowler, of Galveston, and George Jordan, Eber W. Cave, Abram Groesbeeck, and A. S. Richardson, of Houston. Named as officers were Whitney, president; Jordan, vice president; Cave, treasurer; and Richardson, secretary. Fowler, Cave, and Richardson were named to the executive committee.

The unsecured creditors met in Houston on May 11 with Whitney, Cave, and Richardson to hear the company proposal for the liquidation of floating debt. Whitney explained there could be no cash settlement, and offered 7 percent, ten-year third-mortgage indemnity bonds as the best the company could do. In a meeting of the creditors presided over by Gustave Ranger of Galveston, the sentiment generally favored acceptance of the bonds over the appointment of a receiver. The group met with Whitney on May 16 and informed him of their acceptance. The suit filed in Austin was dropped, and Morgan paid numerous debts with transfers from his other enterprises. Most of the refinancing of the company was completed by September, and by October the company's credit was reported to be sound. According to Morgan biographer James P. Baughman, the purchase gave a new focus to Morgan's land-sea network, with Hous-

ton connected to the interior and to Louisiana first by steamship and ultimately by railroad track. He improved his competitive position with the
railroads entering Texas from the north as well as with the Mallory ships
running between Galveston and New York. "All in all, then, the H&TC
was a calculated risk which brought Morgan closer to his goal of a network of railroads and steamships linking the Southwest with Mexico,
Cuba and the East," concluded Baugham.[43]

For the remainder of the 1870s the H&TC functioned as part of the
Morgan system, officially known as the Morgan Louisiana & Texas Railroad & Steamship Company (ML&TR&S). Morgan's death on May 8,
1878, made little difference in the plans and management of the company
since Charles Whitney, who was also his son-in-law, had been well
trained to assume leadership. Texas law prohibited consolidation of the
H&TC, as well as the Gulf, Western Texas & Pacific Railroad between
Indianola and Cuero, but stock ownership and interlocking directorates
insured a community of interests between the elements of the transportation empire. As Baugham described it, "The Morgan strategy called
for the H&TC to blanket the area north of the Colorado and west of the
Trinity rivers, channeling imports and exports of this region via Houston [Clinton] and the Morgan steamers, and commanding substantial
pro rata share of the traffic between Texas points and Kansas City and
St. Louis via its connection with the Missouri, Kansas & Texas." On
May 28, 1879, the H&TC incorporated the new Texas Central Railway,
which would build across Central Texas from Ross near the mainline to
Cisco and Albany in West Texas. The net earning power of the H&TC was
a disappointment to the Morgan officials, but the combined earning and
borrowing power of the ML&TR&S was able to keep the road solvent. Not
a totally satisfactory situation, it was not to last very long: the entire railroad picture of Texas and Louisiana would begin to change in the 1880s
with the entrance of Gould and Huntington to the area.[44]

Galveston weathered the storms of the 1870s, but even greater threats
and challenges lay ahead. First, however, let us examine the experiences of
the Gulf, Colorado & Santa Fe during the 1870s.

CHAPTER TWO

GALVESTON'S OWN
RAILROAD EMERGES

On May 9, 1873, the *Galveston Daily News* announced on its front page that a bill had been introduced in the state legislature to charter a new railroad company, the Gulf, Colorado & Santa Fe, from Galveston across the Brazos River, then northwest across Texas to Santa Fe, New Mexico. Near Eastland it would cross Thomas A. Scott's Texas & Pacific, building west to California, and at Santa Fe it would connect with the Denver & Rio Grande Railway. The full text of the proposed act was published, naming the commissioners, authorizing the sale of stock, detailing the route, and spelling out the other obligations and privileges typical of such incorporation legislation.[1]

About half of the commissioners named were well-known Galveston businessmen: Albert Somerville, Peter J. Willis, John L. Darragh, Leon Blum, A. C. McKeen, Nahor B. Yard, George Lawrence, Moritz Kopperl, John S. Sellers, Dr. William R. Smith, and C. E. Broussard. The remainder, such as Moses Austin Bryan of Brazoria County, a nephew of Stephen F. Austin, and B. H. Basset of Brenham, were businessmen from towns along the proposed route who would be instrumental in obtaining subscriptions for stock.[2]

Obviously, planning had taken place in order to get the legislation drafted and commissioners selected. Some thought had been given to the route. However, the announcement of the introduction of the legislation was not preceded by months of citizen meetings and wrangling as occurred in previous years. Unfortunately, it is not known what the planning process was and exactly who the key players were who brought it about. Several of the incorporators—Somerville, Smith, McKeen, Blum, Kopperl, and Sellers—had been involved with the Galveston, Houston & Henderson or the series of citizens meetings on railroad matters in 1871, so their experience and familiarity with the previous work may have been used in planning the GC&SF.

A meeting of the incorporators on May 12, 1873, indicates how some of the previous planning may have occurred. The incorporators—John H. Hutchings, George B. Nichols, Waters S. Davis, J. F. Barnett, T. J. Davis, John Sealy, B. R. Davis, R. H. Wynne, W. W. Upham, T. Camp, Charles Schmidt, and George Lawrence—passed a resolution urging the legislature to act swiftly on the proposed GC&SF charter. However, the incorporators feared that the existence of a previous charter still in effect for a "Galveston & Colorado Railroad," issued May 16, 1871, might cause a problem with the legislature. That charter approved a route heading west from Galveston to Columbia and a connection with the Galveston, Harrisburg & San Antonio. In view of this circumstance, five incorporators of the Galveston & Colorado drafted a petition to the legislature recommending the approval of the Gulf, Colorado & Santa Fe, and Waters Davis, Hutchings, Sealy, B. R. Davis, and Lawrence signed it. Also, the Galveston & Colorado was approved in the time period that Caleb Forshey was recommending a new road from Galveston to West Texas and the Pacific Ocean. It is possible that incorporators of the first road worked with Forshey on the plans for it, and that some residue from this effort was passed on to the incorporators of the Gulf, Colorado & Santa Fe.[3]

Or perhaps the impetus for the second road was provided by Thomas A. Scott's plans for the Texas & Pacific Railroad. Scott was anxiously looking forward to the completion of the GC&SF so that materials and supplies needed for the building of the Texas & Pacific across West Texas could be carried over it. A press report pointed out the advantage to Galveston of having the connection to San Diego by way of the T&P, with Galveston serving as the Gulf terminus for freight from San Diego. Whether Scott specifically encouraged this aspect was not indicated, although he had discussed his options of making either Galveston or New Orleans the Gulf terminus of the T&P. It did not matter; Galveston resolved the issue for him by planning a connecting line.[4]

The legislature approved the charter on May 28, 1873, and the commissioners met on June 19 to begin seeking stock subscriptions. Somerville presided, and Bassett acted as secretary. The first action was to increase the number of commissioners by adding James M. Brown, Henry Rosenberg, J. T. Harcourt, John D. Rogers, William L. Moody, Guy M. Bryan, H. Miller, and John Adriance. Considerable discussion revolved around William K. Little's desire to be named general agent in order to seek subscriptions from northern capitalists, a process he had already begun under the assumption that he would be named. Several members objected to the idea of soliciting in the North, believing that the local sources should be exhausted first in order to maintain as much local control as possible. The other major issue was appropriate procedure, which called for the commissioners to step aside once $200,000 of stock had been subscribed and for the stockholders then to elect directors of the company. On the first day of subscriptions, among the smaller businessmen along The Strand, $80,000 was taken.[5]

One of the commissioners, William K. Little, wrote a letter to the editor that appeared on the front page of the *Daily News,* shedding some light on the planning process for the GC&SF and the preparation of the legislation. Little, who was losing the key role that he had cut out for himself, defended himself against the *News's* earlier charge that he was "seeking a fat sinecure." First, he pointed out how the naming of an agent to handle subscriptions until a board of directors could be elected was actually provided for by specific language in the legislation. Second, he claimed that he wrote the legislation, secured its passage through the legislature with no help from Galveston interests, obtained the incorporators, and located northern investors ready to buy, all without the help of the *Galveston Daily News.* He insisted that, after hearing of Scott's plans, he favored the road for the very same reasons that the *Daily News* had—a direct route to the Gulf from San Diego, and a means of obtaining materials and supplies for Scott's T&P through the port of Galveston. He recommended a financing plan for acquiring the initial $2,000,000 from the citizens and government of the city of Galveston and the counties along the line, with the balance provided by "the parties building the road." He also claimed that his plans were based upon his practical railroad experience and advice obtained from other practical men whom he consulted. But Little's northern investors did not fit into Galveston's plans.[6]

On July 11, 1873, the commissioners announced that the $200,000 in stock subscriptions required to organize and elect directors had been raised. The anticipated subscriptions by the large businesses were supplemented by a significant effort on the part of small businesses, with employees buying whatever they could afford. In contrast to the other railroad proposals that failed in spite of considerable drum-beating, the GC&SF sparked a public response that probably astounded everyone. Campaigns for the other roads were heavily supported but failed; this one had actually raised $200,000 from the citizens within two months of its announcement.[7]

Unlike with previous proposals where the *Galveston Daily News* had to devote considerable editorial space to explaining all of the advantages to the citizens, letters of support for this proposal, from readers using such pen names as "Progress," "Q," and "Verite," extolled the virtues of the GC&SF. They called attention to the mineral resources, both in New

Mexico, Arizona, and California along the T&P route, and in Colorado along the route of the Denver & El Paso Railroad. The GC&SF stood to receive an enormous traffic of these ores. Much of this ore had to be shipped to Europe for reduction, and mining interests looked forward to a direct route from the mines to the Gulf by way of the GC&SF. Closer to home, the line would pass through the rich sugar- and cotton-producing areas along the coast before turning north and passing through equally rich growing areas in Central Texas. In addition to all of this export trade, there would also be an increase of products for the Galveston market— poultry, vegetables, and fruit.[8]

The stockholders met on September 13, 1873, and, lacking a quorum, resolved to meet again October 13 to organize and elect officers in accordance with the charter. Quarantine conditions interfered with obtaining a quorum for the October meeting also, but by that time much more serious problems had arisen to interfere with the progress of the new road. The reckless speculation in railroads and wholesale stock watering in many industries, coupled with widespread corruption in government, created precarious economic conditions in 1873.[9]

SEVERE DEPRESSION SETS IN

By the end of August twenty-five railroads had defaulted on their interest payments, causing the bond market to turn sour. The largest investment banking firm of the time, Jay Cooke and Company, the financiers of the Union in the Civil War, was unable to sell the bonds of the Northern Pacific Railroad and financed them with short-term deposits. Unfortunately, the economic situation in Europe was also precarious. When a financial panic in Vienna caused investors there to unload American stocks and bonds, Cooke and Company, caught short, went bankrupt on September 18, 1873, and the stock market was forced to close for ten days. The worst of all things for a new enterprise had happened—a major economic depression. The Panic of 1873 started a depression that would last for six years. Railroads were the worst hit. Eventually eighty-nine defaulted on their bonds, construction ceased, and by 1874, 500,000 men were out of work. There were 6,000 commercial failures in 1874, almost 8,000 in 1875, and more than 9,000 in 1876. The effect rippled throughout the economy. Supply industries suffered, as well as industries that relied upon the railroads for transportation. The overproduction of crops in the rapidly expanding West also suffered when, following the Franco-Prussian War, exports could not bring satisfactory prices. It was against this backdrop of economic and financial chaos that the GC&SF would have to struggle not only to grow but merely to survive.[10]

The stockholders proceeded with their organization and elected the first board of directors on November 14, 1873. Named were Moritz Kopperl, Richard S. Willis, William L. Moody, Albert Somerville, A. C. Crawford, James Sorley, Henry Rosenberg, D. Theodore Ayers, B. H. Bassett, John Sealy, I. H. Catlin, Thomas F. Hudson, and J. Condiet Smith. The board met to elect officers on November 26, 1873, and named Somerville president and Kopperl vice president. Understandably, the full impact of the failure of Cooke and Company and the surrounding events was not yet clear, and the reportage of the meeting reflected the optimism of the time:

> These gentlemen have no superiors in the State as far as business capacity, energy, and indomitable pluck go, and if they can not build the contemplated road it will be useless for anybody else to try.
> The stockholders of the road are to be complimented on the choice of officers made; they have the confidence of the public, and immediate action may be expected.[11]

Once the Galveston County Commissioners voted to issue $500,000 in bonds to buy stock and the state of Texas granted sixteen sections of public land for each mile built, the company was in a position to start building. General Braxton Bragg of Civil War fame was named chief engineer, and he in turn hired J. P. Fresenius to head a survey party for the first 150 miles. Henry Rosenberg was elected president in December, 1874, and in the spring of 1875 bids were solicited and a contract was awarded to Burnett and Kilpatrick to start work. A groundbreaking was held May 1, 1875, and work began the next month. In June, Fresenius replaced Bragg and was greeted in September by a hurricane that caused delay while track and the bay bridge were repaired. Financial problems were persistent during the next two years, and only forty-five miles of track were laid.[12]

The GC&SF was to lead a very turbulent life throughout the remainder of the 1870s before eventually declaring bankruptcy. In addition to the Panic, two other problems plagued the company. The lack of experienced management—executives with railroad backgrounds and the time to devote to the task—was the first. That problem was not unique: other new railroads faced the same dilemma. The other problem, however, was somewhat unique. When the Galveston County Commissioners Court voted to provide $500,000, the commissioners bought voting stock instead of making a donation. Most governmental entities at that time donated cash, land, or materials in order to have the railroads built. Thus when the Santa Fe sold $750,000 worth of stock, two-thirds belonged to the county, giving the commissioners a voting majority over the private stockholders. Both problems would come to the forefront in 1877 and are worth exploring in some detail because of their impact on the company.

GC&SF, COUNTY ARE CRITICIZED

Although the construction proceeded to achieve the first forty-five miles, the pace of the progress beyond that point, as well as some other matters, gave rise to discontent in some quarters. On August 10, 1877, the *Daily News* carried a letter to the editor signed "Citizen"[13] that sharply criticized the management of the GC&SF for its failures and attacked the county commissioners court for not protecting the investment of the taxpayers of Galveston County. In addition to wanting facts on the costs of the completed road and comparisons of these costs with those of other railroads, "Citizen" wanted to know why the GC&SF bridge was built on the north side of the GH&H bridge, a factor that caused it to suffer damage in the September, 1875, hurricane, or why it was built at all instead of using the GH&H bridge, which had been built by the city of Galveston in the first place. He also attacked the GC&SF for its "road to nowhere," ending in a prairie when it should have been built without any delay to the connection with the GH&SA, opening the direct line to San Antonio. The last charge questioned the motives and even the integrity of the directors. "Citizen" asked, "Does the present directory, with the tacit consent of the guardians of the people's interest [i.e., the county commissioners court], intend to allow the road to go to apparent ruins, and then at an auspicious moment gobble up and seize the valuable franchise for their own individual benefit, leaving the county to hold the bag, as did the city on a similar occasion with the Wharf Company?" The idea of deliberate bankruptcy was not uncommon in the days of the freewheeling finances of the Gilded Age.[14] In fact, the GC&SF was only two years away from bankruptcy at the time of "Citizen's" complaint, and there is an ominous tone to his question. Is it a "question" or a "forecast"? Having once addressed his queries to President Rosenberg to no avail, he this time directly challenged the county judge and the commissioners to respond.[15]

The following day County Judge William H. Williams replied to the complaints against him and the commissioners in a lengthy interview. Here it was revealed that a serious issue had arisen between the court and the directory of the GC&SF regarding the future construction of the road.

In July the GC&SF had received a "communication" from T. H. Dockery regarding the building of the road to Belton. President Rosenberg would not discuss the matter, but other directors claimed that Dockery's action did not constitute a proposal, nor did he demonstrate any ability to perform a contract if he submitted a proposal that was accepted. However, Dockery also presented his "communication" to the county court, which judged it to be a specific proposal, voted that it should be accepted, and, through Commissioner John H. Hurt, informed the board of directors.

Judge Williams described the events at the meeting: "The question of Dockery's proposal was brought up, which irritated Mr. President Rosenberg, who said a great many things that were suggested by his feelings and opinions about it, and among others, he said that he cared nothing for the people's interest in the road, that the directory would go on and build five miles more of the road and would then come forward and demand the $50,000 for this work from the county." Judge Williams stated that Commissioner Hurt took exception to these remarks and suggested that the county might require the GC&SF to show both their ability and inclination to complete the road to the point indicated in the charter before the final $50,000 of county funds would be paid to the GC&SF. At that point, according to Williams, GC&SF vice president Richard S. Willis announced that the attorneys for Dockery, Messrs. Willie and Cleveland, instructed him to withdraw the proposal from consideration. That, of course, ended the matter, but Judge Williams said he was then disposed to question Dockery's action when he knew that the county court controlled the majority of the stock in the road and had approved his proposal. Judge Williams also pointed out that the state of Texas had given the road land certificates for 460,800 acres of public domain, and that the county bonds issued for twenty-five years would cost the taxpayers $1,750,000 in principal and interest at maturity—apparently to suggest to President Rosenberg that the public interest in the road was not to be disparaged.[16]

Judge Williams then pointed out that he had always opposed the location of the GC&SF bridge to the north [or northeast] of the existing GH&H bridge across the bay to Virginia Point. He recalled that in a board meeting he had said "that the ideas of a certain [Board] member who was a large shareholder in the other road [GH&H] ought not to prevail simply because he wanted some protection to the bridge in which he was largely interested."[17] He told the GC&SF directors that their theory would prove "worse in execution than it promised in its inception." As for "Citizen's" opinion about the intentions of the GC&SF directory, Judge Williams stated, "there is a conspiracy in the directory that has for its object the repudiation of the public's rights and a well defined intention to so legislate over the destinies of this road as will enable the members at the proper moment to come in and with greedy hands gobble up all that the county has contributed to the construction of this road, and while the people are 'whistling down the winds' for their interests the conspirators will rise to the surface and proclaim themselves the master of the situation and of the road."[18]

Rosenberg fired back in an interview of his own the next day, denying most of what Judge Williams stated, especially the remark pertaining to not caring about the public interest. Rosenberg explained that it was his plain duty to serve the interest of the enterprise of which he was the head but that he would resign if the directory had any intentions but to build the road as prescribed in the charter of the company. He also corrected Judge Williams's report on the purpose and sequence of the events at the GC&SF board meeting attended by Commissioner Hurt.

The meeting, he said, had been called to continue consideration of the building of the next five miles of track and the bridge over the Brazos River. On the subject of Dockery, Judge Williams stated that Dockery himself called on him while the board was in session and withdrew the so-called proposal, and that there was nothing to discuss. The subject returned again to the five-mile extension; Hurt, asked for his opinion, expressed his thoughts pertaining to the $50,000 that Judge Williams related. Rosenberg repeated that there was absolutely no question that the company would build the road as contemplated and that another $50,000 was not the issue.

Rosenberg said that he suggested the meeting adjourn until "some time when less feeling was likely to be manifested," at which time Commissioner William J. Jones stated that the county was obligated to pay the $50,000 to the GC&SF when the next five miles was completed and that he would make it his business to see that it happened. Upon this the board of directors voted to go ahead with the five-mile extension and the Brazos Bridge. At the next regular board meeting on September 10, 1877, Rosenberg announced that the firm of Burkett & Burnes had been selected for the construction of the tenth five-mile segment, but no action was taken on the contractor for the bridge.[19]

CONTROVERSY OVER GENERAL BRAGG

President Rosenberg's remarks helped straighten out what occurred at the meeting, especially comments attributed to him. These remarks probably did little to allay the concerns of those looking for the plans for building to Belton and beyond. And his remarks about the positioning of the Galveston Bay Bridge opened a whole new controversy. His statement that chief engineer General Bragg and assistant engineer Fresenius had recommended the position northeast of the GH&H bridge brought forth a long letter from attorney John Lovejoy of the firm of Sayles & Lovejoy, claiming to have a paper written by Bragg, who had died in Galveston on September 26, 1876, stating that he had recommended just the opposite but had been overridden by the board of directors. Bragg had also expressed his differences with Sealy in a letter to his wife, accusing John Sealy of "making it [the GC&SF bridge] a breakwater to the Houston [GH&H] road."[20]

In spite of his questionable record in the Civil War, Bragg had been honored with full military services in Galveston prior to the shipment of his body to Mobile for burial there. To have impugned the memory of a hero of the Battles of Monterrey and Buena Vista in the Mexican War and the Confederate victor at Chickamauga was not the smartest move that Rosenberg could have made in a southern city at that time. Lovejoy wrote:

> How well it sounds. What a eulogy upon Gen. Bragg!
>
> How compatible with Mr. Rosenberg's great soul and benign spirit to speak so well of the honored dead as to lead—if his declarations were true—the world of engineers to hiss his great name and the citizens of Galveston to laugh at his abilities and condemn his memory to ignominy and shame!

Lovejoy went on the explain that Bragg had shared office space with Sayles & Lovejoy for sixteen months prior to his death while Bragg was the state railroad inspector and that he had become very familiar with the history of the GC&SF. Bragg left a detailed daily record of events as well as the statement regarding the bridge decision. According to Lovejoy, Rosenberg told Bragg that he "presumed to veto the choice of his own officers," thus placing the bridge in position to sustain the $25,000 in damages that it suffered in the storm of September, 1875. After additional condemnation of Rosenberg, Lovejoy's letter challenged him directly: "We want answers to the questions of 'Citizen,' and these must come, or the people will consign those who refuse to a suitable obscurity."[21]

Having become aware of the diary left by General Bragg, the *Galveston Daily News* chose not to let the matter rest and published two excerpts, one for the period October 8, 1874, through April 30, 1875, and another for the period May 6, 1875, through June 17, 1875, when Bragg was relieved and filed a lawsuit against the company. Bragg has been described as intelligent and energetic with a stern sense of duty, but he also was quarrelsome and irritable. Therefore, his diary entries must not always be taken as objective and well thought out. Nevertheless, in total they do present an inside view of the management system and style of the company in its first years. The thirteen-man board of directors was composed of bankers, lawyers, merchants, and cotton factors. It can be assumed that all were versed in the practices of capitalism, finance, and management, although not in a railroad or engineering environment. All were fully occupied with their businesses yet attempted to function as a committee of the whole to manage the GC&SF. There were no full-time executives. General Bragg was not treated as a member of management, and meetings were held without him, which doubtlessly irritated him. He was also irritated when meetings were postponed for lack of a quorum of the directors, once when the opera was in town. (Board meetings were generally in the evenings.)

By April, 1875, his diary records the presence of an executive committee, composed of "S, S, and S" (Albert Somerville, John Sealy, and James Sorley). The function of the executive committee and the reason President Rosenberg was not on it were not explained in the diary. Often decisions were reversed and directions changed, but this probably was not too unusual for any organization in a start-up phase. At one point Bragg named the conflicting factions on the board the "go-ahead" and the "wait and see" men. Later one of the factions, probably the "wait and see" men, was labeled the "know-nothings" by the impatient chief engineer. Bragg also frequently entered charges of false economy against the directors in his diary, although this may have occurred when he thought the directors were either doing his job or ignoring his opinion. There were numerous instances of what Bragg described confusion among the directors, conflicting orders, and duplicate responsibilities being assigned, all of which should have been understandable, though aggravating, to a general accustomed to the confusion of war. As his tenure neared its end, he at one point made an entry complaining that "another ring [i.e., conspiracy] of corner grog-shop engineers have captured Mr. Rosenberg on the economical shake." Once he remarked that a director who was also the agent for the supplier of cross-ties complained that the inspection of the arriving ties was too rigid. Finally he became aware of the conspiracy among some directors to replace him with Fresenius, and recorded that he had turned his papers and his whole claim against the GC&SF over to his attorneys, Ballinger, Jack & Mott.[22]

While some of General Bragg's critical comments may be attributed to his irritable personality and others to the military's dislike for civilian "dis-

orderliness," there is no doubt that the GC&SF had management problems, and the fact that it had built only forty-five miles of track in four
years could not be completely blamed on financial difficulties. Although
the general died almost a year before "Citizen" published his letter attack-
ing the GC&SF management, it may well have been that he voiced his
opinions to outsiders when he was alive and contributed to the dissatis-
faction voiced by "Citizen." One thing is certain: the publication of his diary at the time of the controversy aroused by "Citizen's" letter and Judge
Williams's comments added more fuel to the fire on which the GC&SF
management was already sitting.

CHAPTER THREE

THE PATH INTO
BANKRUPTCY — AND OUT

The GC&SF management controversy served to impress upon County Judge William H. Williams and the commissioners the full meaning of their responsibilities to the taxpayers. Consequently, the impact of the county ownership of the majority of the stock was felt at the October 1, 1877, meeting when Judge Williams decided to vote on all thirteen director positions. This move provoked another controversy that lasted until the December 15, 1877, meeting. At that time members were elected upon the basis of an eight-five split, eight representing the county stock and five representing the private stockholders. At one point during the controversy there were two elected boards, one elected by the commissioners court and the other by the private stockholders, until one resigned so that a compromise could be reached. The squabble also produced a report by the "old board" justifying all of its actions, intended to convince the critics that they were right all along. By December, however, all participants seemed weary of the arguments and wanted to resume progress. The new GC&SF board met on December 16, 1877, and elected Moritz Kopperl president. He immediately launched a campaign to raise $200,000 so that construction could continue to Brenham.[1]

President Kopperl launched into the New Year, 1878, full of vigor and optimism, determined that the company would now get on the road to success. The campaign to sell the first $200,000 in company bonds locally before putting them up for sale in New York would surely succeed, he announced. The campaign began quickly, with a citizens' meeting on Wednesday, January 2. When less than two dozen showed up instead of the hundreds expected, the directors saw the first sign of trouble.

The impact of the Panic of 1873 was still being felt in Galveston, and the efforts to sell the bonds were only partially successful. Nevertheless, a contract for grading to the 80-mile post was awarded, as the matter of completing that track by November 28, 1878, as required by the charter, was becoming more of a problem. Dennistoun, Cross & Company (DC&C) of London was approached for financing, but their terms required not only their appointing a majority of the directors but also the county relinquishing its rights. The October 1, 1878, stockholders meeting arrived, and the company announced that the 50-mile post would be reached on the next day, Richmond would be reached by the end of October, and the 80-mile post by the charter deadline. Difficulties with DC&C were not mentioned. The county commissioners made their inspection of the 50 miles on October 19, 1878, and issued the final $50,000 installment of county bonds, bringing the total to $500,000. However, by October 30, the GC&SF's debt reached $162,000, and on November 1 all negotiations with DC&C were terminated.[2]

The flow of critical letters to the *Daily News* continued, precipitating a letter from "Citizen," once the road's strongest critic, who not only defended the GC&SF directors but also attacked the correspondents, stating that their arguments seemed to reflect the views of the H&TC and the Galveston, Harrisburg & San Antonio railroads, the Morgan company, and the interests of Houston. He also implied that all of the letters may have come from a single source. While admitting that he had previously criticized the directors for what the called honest mistakes, he never impugned the integrity of the board in the manner found in the recent letters, which implied that some directors would receive part of the proposed loan.[3]

A front-page editorial on December 10, 1878, addressed another criticism being made in recent letters, including one in the same issue from "Taxpayer." The charge was that the directors were allowing the road to default on the mortgage and forcing it into a bankruptcy sale at which they could purchase it. Ironically, this was an eventuality that "Citizen" had first suggested in his critical letter of August 10, 1877. Now others were suggesting the same outcome. The editorial addressed this charge at length. It recognized that the charge might turn out to be true but added that such a development would at least keep the road alive and under the control of Galveston. After all, if the road were put up for sale, it would be a public sale in which the directors would have to bid against any other parties that may be interested. The editorial also pointed out that the critics were not offering any other solution that would keep the company alive.

THE DIRECTORS SEEK A LOAN

With tension building for the December 14 meeting of the stockholders to vote upon a $250,000 loan, the members of the county court, who of course held the majority vote, were interviewed for indications of how they would vote. This was particularly important because three new commissioners, N. O. Lauve, Thomas Goggan, and John H. Frisby, were elected in November, along with County Judge William H. Williams and Commissioner William J. Jones, who were reelected. However, each member of the court saw the situation as "something vs. nothing," and felt that there was nothing to do but approve the loan if the county was to ever have the benefit of a road that Galveston could control to a rich part of Texas.[4]

The directory met December 14, 1878, to open bids on the $250,000 loan. After advertising in the *New York Journal of Commerce* and the *Boston Post* for bids, the only proposal received was from George Sealy, representing a syndicate of Galveston businessmen, most of whom were already stockholders and directors. The money would be loaned for ninety days at a rate of 12 percent, and the loan would be secured by a deed of trust for all of the track and equipment of the company. Robert Mills was named as trustee. Those participating in the loan were Ball, Hutchings & Company; Moritz Kopperl; J. J. Hendley, Somerville & Davis; Richard S. Willis; Henry Rosenberg; Moody & Jemison; Wallis, Landes & Company; H. Kempner; Charles E. Richards; Sampson Heidenheimer; Isadore Dyer; Julius Runge; LeGierse & Company; John D. Rogers; and Leon & H. Blum Co. Sealy's proposal also included a clause that allowed stockholders to join the syndicate upon their acceptance of the proposal. Later that same day GC&SF attorneys William P. Ballinger and George Flournoy presented the Sealy proposal to the county commissioners court and reviewed its provisions. The court voted unanimously to approve the loan and appointed a committee of Lauve, Goggan, and Frisby to attend the stockholders meeting and to vote in favor of the loan.[5]

The stockholders met on the following day and unanimously approved the loan. The *Galveston Daily News* proclaimed the action as a major historical milestone in another front-page editorial: "The unanimous vote at the meeting of the stockholders of the Gulf, Colorado and Santa Fe road, accepting the proposition of Mr. Geo. Sealy and his co-subscribers to a ninety-day loan of $250,000, is an act that has surmounted a crisis of peculiar peril in the history of Galveston, and planted the standard of progress on firm and rising ground beyond a gloomy chasm of doubts and misgivings, discords and distractions." The *Daily News* saw much of moral value in the action, with many elements of the community coming together to promote the interests of all. After the turmoil and crisis of the previous three months, "something" in the form of a ninety-day loan was a cause for celebration, given the alternative of lawsuits by the contractors, the Baldwin company, the manufacturer of the locomotives, and other creditors.[6]

The first move on the part of the directors after signing the mortgage was to request the county commissioners court to sell its stock in the company. Since the provisions for the county to own stock were contained in the charter approved by the legislature, the first step necessarily involved remedial action by the legislature. On January 19, 1879, GC&SF director Walter Gresham presented to the county court for its approval proposed legislation to permit the county to sell its stock and use the money received to redeem the county bonds issued to support the road. The removal of the county as stockholder in the company would, of course, eliminate the legal problem that caused DC&C to halt the negotiations. All of the court members expressed their desire to see the road built and to aid the selling of the first mortgage bonds. Therefore, they voted unanimously to support the proposed legislation and named Commissioners Lauve and Goggan to confer with the GC&SF directors on the best means of having it passed in the legislature. Two months later Gresham was back to the court with the act passed to open negotiations for the sale. The only new provision in the final act was an obligation on the purchasers to execute a bond for $200,000 that the road to Belton would be built in four years. As might be expected, Gresham was interested in the stock being sold to the current stockholders or mortgage holders. He admitted there were potential buyers in Galveston who would pay more for the county stock in order to stymie the building of the road and eliminate it as a competitor. Marcus F. Mott appeared at the meeting as a private citizen and spoke of the benefits, already well understood, that would accrue to the city and the county if the road to Belton was built as a competitor to the H&TC and the GH&SA roads, forcing Morgan company to ship cotton from Galveston and abandoning plans to bypass Galveston. Judge Williams said he placed the value of the county stock at $10,000. Although the county originally paid $500,000 for this stock, the county and the private stockholders were facing the very real prospect of all stock becoming completely valueless if the company defaulted on its current loan. Commissioner Lauve went even further than Williams; he favored making a present of the stock to any party that would guarantee the completion of the road to Belton.[7]

SEALY'S SYNDICATE BUYS GC&SF

Two days later, March 14, 1879, the county commissioners court met again to consider the sale, and Gresham presented a proposal from a syndicate represented by George Sealy, the same group that held the $250,000 first mortgage, offered the county $10,000 for its stock, and included the bond of $200,000 guaranteeing that the road to Belton would be completed in four years. The court voted to approve Commissioner Frisby's motion to accept the Sealy proposal, with only Commissioner Goggan voting no on the grounds that the court should take more time to make the decision. The court discussed the four-year time limit for completion. Commissioner Lauve considered it too long, but President Kopperl and Flournoy maintained that the four-year limit would ease the sale of mortgage bonds. Gresham said the company would move to build as rapidly as possible, but that the friends of the road in the legislature preferred the longer time, probably to avoid the necessity of coming back to amend the bill that passed. With the elimination of the problem presented by county ownership and control, the *Daily News* optimistically reported: "The whole interest of the road is now in the hands of Galvestonians; the legislature has passed the enabling acts required, and there appears to be no obstacle now in the way of the syndicate getting a loan either in the east or Europe, which will enable them to build the road to Belton. Mr. Kopperl, its president, has now the gratification of success, which is well deserved."[8]

Evidently the public, or at least the *Daily News,* was in the dark regarding the financial condition of the GC&SF: the deadline for the loan, March 16, 1879, arrived, and the company was unable to meet the payment. Consequently, the trustee, Robert Mills, immediately announced the sale of the company on April 15, 1879, to satisfy the loan.[9] Directors met on April 8 and voted to request an extension of the loan deadline. If the extension was granted, they hoped to obtain an additional $500,000 loan and build to Brenham, but the request was turned down by the Sealy syndicate, many of whom were also directors. Without any other options for the directors to pursue, the sale was held as announced. There were only two bidders, A. J. Walker and George Sealy, representing the same the syndicate of investors who made the $250,000 loan. In addition to those previously named, Walter Gresham, Morris Lasker, and William F. Ladd had joined the syndicate. The first bid was Walker's for $50,000, followed by Sealy's for $60,000. The bidding was run up to $200,000 before the sale was awarded to Sealy. Trustee Mills reported the results of the sale to the board on April 17, and a resolution was passed turning the company and all of its assets over to the purchaser and his associates. With that act, the original GC&SF Railway Company and its stock passed into history.

For the *Daily News* it was an occasion for celebration: "The gentlemen into whose hands the road has passed are possessed of large means and almost unlimited credit. They are identified most materially with the city and its immediate surroundings, and may be expected to push the enterprise they have assumed with all possible dispatch."[10] The outcome of the events over the previous six months followed the scenario described by "Citizen," Thomas P. Ochiltree, in his letter published in August, 1877. The GC&SF went into bankruptcy and was purchased at a fraction of its total worth by a small group of stockholders who could now manage it to suit their own personal benefit. However, at this point neither Ochiltree nor the county commissioners nor the *Galveston Daily News* were criticizing the sale. Most of the stockholders who did not join the Sealy syndicate owned very small amounts and lost very little in the foreclosure and sale. The big holders joined the syndicate to make the $250,000 loan and the $200,000 purchase, all of which went to pay off the loan. On the surface, it appears that a financial scheme common to many railroads, as Ochiltree had pointed out earlier, was planned and carried out. But the railroad was still alive, in the hands of Galveston businessmen with the wealth and determination to complete it, and the taxpayers of Galveston County still had hopes of seeing their $500,000 investment paying off in an asset that was going to be of economic benefit to the entire citizenry.[11]

The new owners acted quickly to organize, meeting on April 19 to adopt Articles of Association under the name of the Gulf, Colorado & Santa Fe Railway Company. The articles made it clear that all rights of stockholders in the previous company and all claims against the previous company expired with the April 15 sale. Furthermore, the articles made it clear that the parties to the articles were the only stockholders of the GC&SF Railway Company. The capitalization of the new company, according to the articles, was based upon the amount of money invested prior to the sale, plus an additional amount pledged by the new stockholders.[12]

Once the new directors and officers were in place, things began to happen rapidly. On May 12, 1879, the directors recommended the issuance of first mortgage bonds and the execution of a deed to trust. The stockholders approved the mortgage bonds on May 27, and John S. Kennedy and Charles M. Fry, both of New York, were named trustees. It was soon reported by the finance committee that $540,000 of the bond issue had been subscribed. The board also moved quickly to resume road construction, purchase materials, and push the acquisition of right of way.

RIGHT-OF-WAY ACQUIRED

They also resumed obtaining pledges of support from the counties along the route. Leander Cannon, who had performed this function for the original GC&SF company, and attorney Norman G. Kittrell met with the citizens of Bell County in Belton on June 14, 1879, repeating the arguments regarding the benefits of the railroad to Bell County and reviving the earlier enthusiasm that had been displayed by the citizens there. A resolution introduced by J. W. Embry of Belton was passed renewing the commitments previously made and extending the time limit on them to June 1, 1881, as requested by Cannon. The presence of Walter Gresham and a corps of surveyors in Bellville, located between Richmond and Brenham, was having the effect of waking "the denizens of this old town from their long Rip Van Winkle sleep" and stimulating a small land boom in the area around the proposed depot and the courthouse square, with land selling for $100 to $200 dollars per acre. It was estimated that the population would reach between 1,500 and 3,000 within twelve months. By October the grading of the sixty-three miles from Richmond to Brenham was almost completed, and Gresham informed the citizens of Brenham that the tracks would be completed by Christmas. He also told them that he was acquiring right of way from Brenham to Caldwell and that grading would start soon. On October 11, the board of directors authorized the executive committee to start the work.[13]

The annual stockholders meeting was held October 7, 1879, and the board of directors was reelected. When the directors met on October 30 to elect officers, George Sealy, now forty-four, was elected president to replace his elder brother John, who had become ill. The unfortunate circumstances of the elder Sealy provided the opportunity for the junior partner to take the helm. With management, financial, and legal problems behind him, George Sealy was in a position to move in a dynamic manner, which he did. In late October he announced that repairs to damage to the Brazos Bridge caused by an April flood had been completed, that grading of the road to Richmond was nearing completion, and that contractors Roche and Tierney, who had graded to 12 miles south of Brenham, had taken a contract for grading from Yegua Creek to Caldwell. The track to Richmond reached to within a mile and a half of that city when 600 excursionists crowded on nine passenger cars October 27, 1879, for a trip to that city. In March, 1879, the new GC&SF had the charter amended to require that the 80-mile post be met by March 1, 1880, and the remaining 17 miles past Richmond were now within grasp. From Cameron came news that Walter Gresham, aggressively pursuing his right-of-way activities, had acquired free right-of-way through Milam County to the Bell County line and was in the process of locating a depot in Cameron. Finally, on Christmas Eve President George Sealy announced that the members of the syndicate that purchased the GC&SF on April 15 had increased their subscriptions to $2,500,000. With an appropriate response from the citizens of Belton, said Sealy, the GC&SF would have sufficient means to extend the track to Belton in the coming year.[14]

The end of 1879 found the GC&SF poised for the future. The problems—economic depression, management difficulties, the fight over county control, and bankruptcy—were all behind. The company was now guided by veterans of this period who had learned the business the hard way. President Sealy, who had led the way through the restabilization of the company, was supported by five of the original board members, Vice President Richard S. Willis, Moritz Kopperl, John Sealy, Henry Rosenberg, and William L. Moody. The remaining board members were all men who had been very successful in their own careers, Leon Blum, John D. Rogers, Waters S. Davis, Sampson Heidenheimer, Julius Runge, John C. Wallis, and Walter Gresham. Some of these men had also served as directors during the times of troubles. But now, the learning was behind them, and the management team was ready to pursue higher goals in the coming decade.[15]

CHAPTER FOUR

THE RAPIDLY
CHANGING WEST

In the same manner that Galveston's early growth forty years before had been fostered by the rapid increase in population and cotton production in the valleys of the Brazos and Colorado Rivers of southern Texas, so a new era of growth would be stimulated by the rapid increase in population and grain production in the western states that followed the Civil War. At the same time that the industrial transformation was taking place in the eastern states, another equally important agricultural transformation was taking place in the newly settled western states, where the large increases in grain production occurred at the time when world markets were expanding.

According to historian Richard White, the growth of agriculture and mining in the western states was occurring in combination with a rapid increase in world population, urbanization, improvements in transportation, and European imperialism. Taken together, these causes produced a rapidly escalating demand for basic commodities and an expanding world market centered on Europe and the United States.[1]

In order to develop and take advantage of the favorable circumstances, the West, of course, needed labor and capital. With a basically extractive economy, the West also needed markets for its commodities and a transportation system that could convey these resources to the markets, according to White. He cites the case of wheat, which after 1880 became the major agricultural export of much of the Great Plains, California, and the interior Pacific Northwest. U.S. grain exports had doubled by 1880 and would continue to soar as world population increased by more than 50 percent during the half-century preceding World War I.[2]

Fueled by these transformations, the nation experienced its greatest railroad building in the 1880s. With the effects of the Panic of 1873 behind it, the country began to experience an expanding economy and capital was again available for financing a network of railroads crisscrossing the vast area between the Mississippi River and the Pacific Ocean. Railroad builders laid more than 40,000 miles of track west of the Mississippi during the 1880s, for a total of 72,473 by 1890. States such as Kansas, Nebraska, and Texas nearly tripled their mileage. As the principal tycoons of the railroad industry—Jay Gould of the Missouri Pacific, Collis P. Huntington of the Southern Pacific, Thomas Nickerson and, later, William B. Strong of the Atchison, Topeka & Santa Fe, and General William Palmer of the Denver & Rio Grande—began designing their transcontinental systems, the importance of Galveston as a rail-sea transportation center began to assume new proportions. One after another, these men and their top executives began to visit Galveston to see for themselves the potential the port held and how it might fit into their plans for lacing the western United States and Mexico with a network of rail lines. Galveston's Gulf, Colorado & Santa Fe Railway would be part of this massive building program, and the city, the port, and the railroad would benefit from the convergence of economic factors affecting the world at this time.

The Gilded Age was reaching full bloom as the oil, iron and steel, and railroad industries led the great charge to bring industrialization to the United States. Investment capital was flowing, the accumulation of great wealth—both corporate and personal—was under way, and a new America was in the process of creation. In the West the creation of three large railroad lines, headed by three dynamic individuals, was launched. Gould's Southwestern System—consolidated under the Missouri Pacific—was building from St. Louis to California and Mexico; Huntington's Southern Pacific was building east from California to both rail connections with the Atlantic seaboard and shipping connections with Europe; and the Atchison, Topeka & Santa Fe was preparing to challenge both Gould's Union Pacific and his Missouri Pacific throughout the western United States and Mexico. Texas, with its vast lands, its large cattle industry, its expanding cotton crop, and its new grain fields, lay in the pathway of each of these lines as they developed their strategies for conquering the West and outmaneuvering each other. Each was also conscious of taking advantage of rail-sea connections, and they began to assess the value of Galveston and its fine harbor as a factor in their transcontinental strategies.[3]

Although the real growth in Galveston did not take place until after 1880, there were earlier signs of the change to come and the impact that it might have on Galveston's destiny. As early as 1874, the *Galveston Daily News* had copied articles from the *San Diego Union* and San Francisco's *Alta California* regarding Galveston's potential as a transfer point in a land-sea network that would shorten the route to the ports on both sides of the Atlantic Ocean. At that time the surplus wheat crop of California, ready for export on July 1, 1874, and worth $22,500,000, could have commanded a premium price of $37,500,000 if it could beat the crops of English, continental European, and other American farmers to Liverpool. However, because of the four months required by ship from California, the penalty for arriving last in Liverpool would amount to $7,000,000 or more. The advantages of a railroad over low grades from California to the Texas coast were obvious. The railroad would substantially shorten the time to a port from which ships could take the cargoes to Liverpool. With plans already announced for the controversial Texas & Pacific Railroad to build to California, and for the Gulf, Colorado & Santa Fe to construct a line running northwest from Galveston and intersecting with the Texas & Pacific in West Texas, the California newspapers could see an easy solution to the problems of that state's wheat growers.[4]

The significance of Galveston in the new network of railroads projected was made apparent again in 1878 as a result of the efforts of Thomas A. Scott of Philadelphia. Scott's efforts in Congress to secure a grant were being challenged by Collis P. Huntington of California's Big Four—Leland Stanford, Mark Hopkins, Charles Crocker, and Huntington—who had built the Central Pacific from California in 1869 to meet the Union Pacific at Promontory, Utah, to give the nation its first line to the Pacific Coast. Since then the Four had built other lines that were dominating California and were now focused on a connection to the Texas Gulf Coast that would enable them to transport wheat to the Atlantic Coast and Europe. Huntington offered to build a road east from California and to meet anyone at El Paso. However, he was not interested in Scott's new line, which at that time was projected to build east from Texas to Memphis, Philadelphia, and New York. Huntington was lobbying against Scott before Congress to direct that the federal grant to a line that would meet him at El Paso and connect with Galveston or New Orleans.[5]

The plans generated great excitement across Texas, especially in Galveston, as rumors began to spread. After the economic doldrums caused by the Panic of 1873, the possibilities offered by a network of railroads crisscrossing the state held out the hope of a new era. Soon Huntington, Gould, and other industrialists and financial leaders were visiting the state and making bright forecasts for its future. Texas was set for a decade of very rapid growth, in which population and cotton production would double. Galveston, as the state's largest city and leading seaport, was eager to participate in this expansion. Although by 1890 Galveston would be surpassed by the phenomenal growth of Dallas and San Antonio, the city was poised to play an important role in the expansion as a transportation center. Both Huntington and Gould would be interested in terminal facilities to support their land-sea networks. The Gulf, Colorado & Santa Fe in 1880 was building toward Belton with announced plans to build to Fort Worth. Both Gould and William B. Strong would become interested in purchasing the road to save themselves the time and cost of building to the Gulf. Daily news reports of these plans were eagerly read in Galveston, and real estate values began to rise accordingly.

GRAIN PRODUCTION INCREASES

Whereas wheat production was modest in the eastern and southern states and had leveled off by 1880, 1890 Census statistics indicate that the north-central region, including all of the Great Plains states, increased production by 50 percent (from 194.9 to 329.5 million bushels) between 1880 and 1890, and the western region doubled between 1870 and 1880 (20.9 to 42.9 million bushels) and increased by 50 per cent by 1890 (42.9 to 63.1 million bushels). Overall, wheat production in the United States was 287.7 million bushels in 1870, 459.4 in 1880, and 468.3 in 1890. By 1890 California had become one of the leading states with its crop of 40.8 million bushels, and Kansas had almost doubled its production to 30.4 million bushels and was gaining on the older states east of the Mississippi.[6]

The importance of wheat, of course, had been recognized early in the 1870s when Galveston and Kansas City traded excursions and businessmen of both cities examined the possibilities for trade. The Panic of 1873, grasshopper plagues in the Midwest, and the failure of the railroads promptly to offer what the midwestern grain dealers considered to be competitive rates prevented the rapid expansion of trade envisioned by the excursionists. All was not bleak, however, because a rapid growth of wheat production in Texas in 1875 helped to offset the loss of the Kansas trade. It was estimated by a *Galveston Daily News* reporter who went to investigate that approximately 5,225,000 bushels of small grain, including about 4,000,000 bushels of wheat, had been produced by a band of counties stretching from Travis on the south to Lamar on the north, a geographical region once called the Black Waxy Prairie. In his *Galveston: A History of the Island and the City,* Charles W. Hayes, who probably was the *News* reporter sent to northern Texas, saw the potential for Galveston. Writing in 1879, he observed that if the production of wheat and small grains was responsible for the population growth from 818,579 in 1870 to 2,250,000 in 1878 "it has done more for the general advancement and prosperity of the State than cotton has done for Texas since the days of her independence."[7]

Continuing, he wrote: "If the growing of grain has caused such a wonderful influx into the State what would not the handling and shipping of grain and flour do for Galveston. Instead of having an active season during the few months in which cotton is handled the city would have a prosperous business the year through. No place has become a grain market but has prospered."[8]

Chicago, Kansas City, and San Francisco were cited by Hayes as conspicuous examples of the benefits of the grain trade. "The wheat of California has done more to build up San Francisco, and give her a solid prosperity, than all the gold and silver, or other precious metals that have been or are being dug out of the beds of her streams, or mined from her mountains," wrote Hayes. Undoubtedly, Hayes was aware of the California production numbers and the interest of the Southern Pacific Railroad in a terminal on the Gulf of Mexico as part of a land-sea route to the East Coast and Europe since the *News* had already published reports of that interest. In spite of a want of facilities and a lack of knowledge in the successful handling of grain, Galveston had made some progress since the first grain cargo left the port August 29, 1874, with 12,000 bushels aboard. In 1875–76, receipts totaled 93,502 bushels, with 53,000 bushels being exported and 40,000 retained to supply the home demand, according to Hayes. "This city," Hayes wrote, "cannot ignore the grain trade if she desires to become the leading metropolis of the Southwest."[9]

PREPARATIONS FOR GRAIN

As the grain receipts and exports were increasing, a group of the merchants involved met on July 27, 1876, at the Cotton Exchange for the purpose of organizing a Produce Exchange. Colonel John S. Sellers was elected president, and A. G. Mills was requested to act as secretary. Others present were Charles W. Hurley, James Arbuckle, A. C. Garcia, James P. Evans, W. A. Oliphint, W. K. McAlpine, Charles H. Byrne, Leander Cannon, Edward Webster, and C. O. Bingham. The organization officially took effect on August 8, 1876, and the *Galveston Daily News* commented that the event "marks an important step in the progress working towards the consummation of plans for building up the grain trade, and in effecting, by means of a common center for transaction of general produce business, that concentration which is essential to successful operations."[10] The *News* went on to explain the wisdom of having a Produce Exchange separate from the Cotton Exchange, inasmuch as the cotton factors were representatives of the producers. Thus, cotton brokers were excluded from membership in the Produce Exchange, although it was recognized that they would be very interested in its management.[11]

Soon afterwards the members of the Exchange began planning an excursion to North Texas to start promoting the grain trade and also published an open letter to the people of Galveston. The letter was more than a statement of purpose, however; it was an analysis of Galveston's position in the rapidly changing world of commerce and what was required to prosper: "Commerce knows no pause; it is either progress or decadence; and once on the inclined plane, a sliding down to ruin becomes inevitable."[12] Although the law of trade that said that "commerce seeks the nearest water transportation" had been true in the past and Galveston had prospered by it, the "artificial advantages" of railroads were now overcoming the "natural advantages" offered by water. The penetration of Texas by railroads from the Northeast was under way and would only expand in the future. The letter also noted that "the opening of Buffalo Bayou to seagoing vessels may, or may not, materially affect our trade—time will tell." In addition, the city would have to look to capturing the trade of Brownsville and the South Texas region, then dominated by Charles Morgan's ships, and open two-way commerce with the ports of Mexico and Central and South America. Initial steps in these directions had already been taken, and the letter urged the support of the entire city—merchants, property holders, mechanics, and all—because Galveston was a city that lived by trade and all would benefit, or perish. The letter was signed by the officers of the Produce Exchange: President John S. Sellers; Vice President Charles W. Hurley; Treasurer D. F. Holland; Secretary X. B. DeBray, the former Confederate general who once commanded the defenses at Galveston during the Civil War; and directors A. C. Garcia, B. P. Grigsby, John Hibbert, J. A. Owens, N. H. Ricker, H. C. Stone, Winter Walker, and John Wolston. By November the Exchange was in full operation, posting statistics on a whole range of products in addition to grain and displaying the manifests of railroads and steamers for the convenience of all.[13]

While there certainly were positives in the attitudes of Galveston's business leaders, there were apparently some offsetting negatives in the city's commercial practices. Some of this criticism first surfaced during the excursion by the Exchange members to northern Texas. The excursionists arrived in Denison on August 23, 1876, and the usual welcoming ceremonies and speech making took place. They were to make a short trip into the Indian Territory, then proceed to Sherman, McKinney, Plano, Dallas, and Waco. While the speeches focused on future possibilities, the speakers also paid attention to the facts and figures—carloads shipped and comparative freight rates.

The party arrived in Waco on August 26 and then returned to Galveston. However, on August 29 the *Galveston Daily News* carried a reprint of an editorial from the *Sherman Courier* blasting President Sellers for remarks he made suggesting that Sherman help Denison build another railroad with a connection to the Great Northern toward the Gulf to compete with the Houston & Texas Central. The idea that Sherman, already connected by railroads to St. Louis, Memphis, and New Orleans, had to help build another to Galveston, for Galveston's benefit, was more than the North Texans could bear. In very blunt terms the *Courier* reminded the Galvestonians, who had long neglected commercial relations with North Texas, "that only in their estimation is Galveston the great maelstrom, the center of gravity to which we must all come and pay our tribute, and that outside of Galveston there is no place in Texas worthy of note."[14]

Criticism did not come only from outsiders. When the Produce Exchange formally opened its offices on the Strand in October, banker Henry Seeligson offered the following blunt suggestions:

> Need I dwell upon the requirements of our city, and say to the cotton factors [i.e., commission merchants], cheapen the handling of cotton at your port, return all rebates allowed you to the shippers. Let the cotton brokers in a like manner lend their mite to the public good by a reduction of their brokerage charges. Let the compress follow in the wake by a reduction, placing them on a parity with New Orleans and Mobile. . . . If we expect to retain our business we can only do so upon a basis of competing in the handling of the products of our State as cheaply as it is done at other Southern ports.

Seeligson left no doubts in the minds of his listeners as to the importance of trade in grain and all of the others products of Texas. Pointing out that the six months of cotton activity at the port left both labor and capital idle for the remainder of the year, he emphasized that grain and other products could provide a full twelve months of port activity, a condition that would also enable the banks to lower their interest rates and to correct another of the hindrances to business in Galveston.[15]

While the excursions to the cities to the north were important—both for making the personal contacts between buyers and sellers and for educating the Galveston merchants to the potential that lay within the state's borders—it was obvious that more was necessary for the city and its port to move into a new economic era. With theirs being the major port serving the cotton-producing region of Texas since the earliest days, the merchants at Galveston enjoyed a certain monopoly, and their somewhat arrogant attitude ("Where else can they go?") apparently showed through on the excursion.

This attitude developed in the prewar years, according to historian Earl Fornell, as a result of the natural advantages of Galveston Bay over the other potential port sites on the Texas Gulf Coast. The Wharf Company, controlled by the city's most successful businessmen, exercised its advantage to the utmost, and the other businesses followed its lead.[16] When the Katy and H&TC railroads met at the border between Texas and the Indian Territory near Denison, establishing contact between Kansas City and St. Louis and Texas, the facts of economic life changed.

While attitudes would change slowly, specific steps to promote the grain trade, such as the organization of the Produce Exchange already described and the provision of grain elevators for the loading of the ships, could be taken promptly. According to information contained in the city directories for 1878 and 1881–82, the Galveston Elevator Company, located on Avenue A between Twenty-second and Twenty-third Streets, was in existence in 1875 and was reported to have shipped 61,000 bushels of wheat between September 1, 1875, and August 31, 1876. The Texas Star Flour Mills, located on Avenue A between Twenty-first and Twenty-second Streets, was built in 1877 and 1878 by the Reymershoffer brothers, John and Gus, who had previously been in the crockery and glassware business. The first mill was built on the south side of Avenue A, near the water's edge. After the area north of Avenue A was filled, the company later built a new plant on the new site. The flour mill created a large demand for wheat shipments into Galveston for processing, producing about 100 barrels of flour each day. The company would grow continuously to the point fifty years later where it was requiring between four and five million bushels of wheat per year and producing 5,000 barrels of flour per day. The City Directory for 1880–81 also listed a Galveston Mills on Mechanic between Thirty-first and Thirty-second Streets. Elevators large enough to handle a truly large grain trade would not come until the 1890s when Elevator A at Fourteenth Street and Elevator B at Twenty-ninth Street were constructed.[17]

In the midst of all of this change taking place in Galveston and throughout the West, two of the nation's railroad titans began to extend their empires into Texas and fixed their gaze upon the assets of Galveston. Jay Gould, looking southwest from St. Louis toward Mexico, saw the plains of Texas and the port at Galveston playing a role in his grand scheme. Huntington, having dominated California with the Southern Pacific and

Central Pacific lines, was now looking eastward to connect those lines to his coal mining empire and its port at Newport News, Virginia. He too saw a place for Galveston in his grand scheme.

GOULD'S AIMS IN TEXAS AND MEXICO

Jay Gould's move to the southwest in 1879 represented not only a change in tactics but also a new strategic outlook. Gould was confusing his opponents and critics as he changed directions and began assembling the roads that would comprise his Southwestern System. By 1879, the railroad situation in the nation was changing and Gould was the first to recognize the trend. As biographer Maury Klein described the situation, "The forces had already been unleashed; he was merely the first to harness them to his own purposes. Jay understood . . . that competition had rendered the territorial concept extinct. Too many roads, large and small, crowded against one another and more were coming. . . . In so unsettled a state bold strategists pointed to self-contained systems as the surest refuge."[18]

Gould's presence with the Wabash was disclosed April 22, 1879, when Commodore C. K. Garrison, who had bought the rundown road in November, 1878, resigned as president. Gould-watchers on Wall Street and in the railroad community believed this and other acquisitions in the Midwest were made on behalf of the Union Pacific, which would become the centerpiece of a Gould system stretching from Toledo to Denver. Contrary to the image Gould had built of himself as a speculator, he now "saw himself as a builder, a pioneer of western development, blazing the trail of progress not with the plow but with rails, mines, commerce." The financial editors, taken by surprise, began to question how he would handle his eastern connections, and whether he would deal or fight with Commodore Cornelius Vanderbilt.[19]

After considerable maneuvering that saw him proposing to merge the Kansas Pacific, Union Pacific, and Denver Pacific, among other things, he dropped another surprise. On November 13, 1879, he purchased Garrison's 4,000 shares, half of the stock, in the Missouri Pacific in a $3.8 million deal that included the Kansas Central and another small Kansas road. This was followed by the most sensational deal that Wall Street had yet seen. On November 26, Vanderbilt sold 150,000 of his shares in the New York Central, with an option for 100,000 more, to a syndicate of J. P. Morgan and Company and Gould and his associates. Financial editors wrote that it signaled an alliance between Gould and Vanderbilt, and one newspaper called it the most powerful railway combination ever known.[20]

Gould's movements had the other railroads both perplexed and fearful. Charles Perkins, president of the Burlington, warned John Forbes, leader of the investment syndicate in Boston, that countercombinations could be formed. Perkins wanted to bring in the Rock Island and the Santa Fe, and Forbes was negotiating for the bankrupt Missouri, Kansas & Texas with its Dutch bondholders.[21]

Again, Gould bought stock quickly and quietly while others fiddled. He dropped another surprise when he was elected president of the Missouri, Kansas & Texas at the stockholders meeting on January 26, 1880, and he promptly announced his plan to connect it with the Texas & Pacific.[22] In fact, before Gould was elected to the Katy presidency, he had already organized a syndicate to extend the Texas & Pacific from Fort Worth to El Paso. With the formation of a construction company to extend the Katy from Denison to Dallas and a connection with the Texas & Pacific, Gould entered not only Texas but the transcontinental railroad wars. With Huntington pushing the Southern Pacific from California to El Paso, and the Santa Fe allying itself with the St. Louis and San Francisco, the Union Pacific was now being threatened with transcontinental competition from two sources. According to Klein, "Gould's moves could thus be interpreted as an attempt to check the expansion of formidable rivals," and as a screen for his real purposes. To Wall Street it appeared that Gould had bought a lot of cheap southwestern stocks in order to run up their price on the market.[23]

Little by little throughout 1880 Gould revealed his plan. First he brought in General Grenville Dodge to run the Texas & Pacific and to build the extensions to El Paso and Denison as well as the link between Texarkana and New Orleans. With Huntington marching toward El Paso, General Dodge announced that construction crews would reach El Paso by January, 1882, a year ahead of the previous schedule. Next Gould revealed his plans to reach the Rio Grande and the Gulf of Mexico. His attention was attracted to the International and Great Northern, destined to reach across the state from Longview to Palestine to San Antonio and eventually to Laredo on the Rio Grande. He also was attracted to the Gulf, Colorado & Santa Fe, which was building from Galveston to Fort Worth and a junction with the Texas & Pacific, thus providing an outlet to the Gulf of Mexico.[24]

In April, 1880, Gould took steps to solidify his control of the Katy, and in June he leased the Katy to the Missouri Pacific without requesting the approval of the bondholders. He quickly announced plans to build extensions to Fort Smith, Arkansas, and Camargo on the Rio Grande, a connecting point to Mexico City. He began to put a squeeze on the St. Louis, Iron Mountain & Southern that resulted in its takeover by December.

The St. Louis, Iron Mountain & Southern, controlled by Thomas Allen, ran from Texarkana to the vicinity of St. Louis, where it connected with a small Illinois line to reach East St. Louis. Thus it was in direct competition with the Katy. First, Gould had the Wabash take over the East St. Louis connection. Then by having both the Texas & Pacific steer traffic to the Katy, and the New Orleans Pacific compete for cotton business, Gould backed Allen into a corner. The last straw came when Gould bought the I&GN in December, cutting off the St. Louis, Iron Mountain & Southern's only remaining feeder. At this point, Allen sold his 40,000 shares to Gould, who acquired 30,000 from other sources and found himself owning almost two-thirds of the St. Louis, Iron Mountain & Southern stock.[25]

GOULD'S SCHEME UNFOLDS

By the end of 1880, what had been a complete mystery to the railroad community began to take shape. Although Gould was still moving in many directions, his expansion into Texas became the one consistent thread. A vast system was emerging, stretching from El Paso to the Gulf. It had also become clear that his system pointed toward St. Louis, where he controlled nearly all of the railroads entering from the West and where his headquarters would be established. Heading a combination that encompassed 8,168 miles of track, the largest amount in the control of any one individual or corporation, Gould emerged as one of the leading railroad men in the country.[26]

Of this accomplishment, Maury Klein writes: "Here at last was what he had been searching for, the task worthy of his talents. His career had been a persistent search for the right challenge to engage his genius to the fullest, as a general seeks the war, the battlefield, that will fulfill his destiny. Jay had found his field and for the rest of his life never let go of it, whatever else he did. It was there for the taking, and above all it was his to take."[27]

As it turned out, the vast expanse of Texas comprised the greater part of the "field," and Galveston, the largest city, the largest seaport, and a business center of the state, would come to play a significant role in Gould's plans. Galveston's place in Gould's plans began to unfold in March, 1881, when Gould made his first visit to Galveston and, in addition to the interest already expressed in the GC&SF, made a proposal to the city to acquire terminal facilities for a Galveston-Vera Cruz steamship line that would be part of his plan for expansion into Mexico. Gould would soon be joined by another very prominent citizen, the former president of the United States, Ulysses S. Grant, who would pay his second visit to Galveston in two years.

The involvement of both Grant and Gould in Mexico began in January, 1880, when Grant, then a potential candidate for another nomination for president by the Republican Party, made a trip to Cuba and Mexico on the advice of political consultants, who felt that it was better if he were out of the country and receiving more of the accolades bestowed upon him during his earlier trip around the world. While in Mexico, he was approached by Matias Romero, a minister in the government of President Porfirio Diaz who was a strong advocate of American investment, Bishop Eulogio Gillow, and Minister of Development Vincente Riva Palacio and asked to publicize in the United States the advantages of Mexican railroad development. On his way back to the United States, Grant paid his first visit to Galveston, arriving on March 23, 1880, aboard the steamship *City of Mexico* from Vera Cruz and departing by train for San Antonio on March 26.[28]

The *City of Mexico* arrived at the outer anchorage and was met by the towboat *Estelle*, the revenue cutter *Louis McLean*, and the steam lighter *S. F. Maddox*. Grant and his party, including his wife, General Phillip H. Sheridan and his wife, Colonel Fred Grant, and others, were transferred to the *Estelle*, where they were met by a greeting party. They were then welcomed at Williams Wharf, where an area had been cordoned off by police for the distinguished guests and welcoming citizens. A twenty-one-gun presidential salute was fired by a detachment from the Galveston Artillery. In close proximity were Mayor Charles Leonard and the welcoming committee, the troops of the Galveston Artillery and the Washington Guards. After words of welcome on the wharf and the boarding of carriages, the procession went through the gates of Williams Wharf onto Twenty-fourth Street, passing a large banner with the inscription "Welcome, Our Guest" floating from an arch composed of cotton bales. The procession reviewed the assembled organizations along Twenty-fourth Street—including firemen, the African-American military company, and local societies—as it moved south to Broadway, where another large banner bearing the words "Welcome to Our Island City" flew from the home of James M. Brown. The procession turned east on Broadway, weaving its way back to the Tremont House hotel, where a large crowd jammed the street. Once inside, a reception lasting several hours was held as people from all walks of life warmly welcomed Grant and his party to Galveston. Following a small dinner, Grant retired to his room, where he greeted delegations from Houston, San Antonio, and Dallas inviting him to add those cities to his visit to Texas.[29]

The next day, Wednesday, March 24, 1880, was highlighted by a sump-

ously, and used the occasion to make the first of his apologetic expla-

one of these newspaper men rushed up to me and'How much to you like Texas?' I was mad, and I said if I owned

Mexican Central Railroad to Thomas Nickerson and the Boston backers of the AT&SF, and the Mexican National Railroad to General Palmer. In October, Mexican minister Matias Romero received a concession and subsidy from the governor of the state of Oaxaca to build a road from Mexico City to the city of Oaxaca. Romero left immediately for the United States, stopping at St. Louis and Chicago on his way to New York, and met with all of the men having interests in the Southwest—Palmer, Nickerson, Dodge, Huntington, and Gould.

On November 11, 1880, Romero entertained Grant and about twenty of the leading railroadmen at Delmonico's famous restaurant, where both he and Grant made speeches praising Mexico as a field for railroad investment. The gathering at Delmonico's, called together by General Grant, included Thomas Nickerson, representing the Mexican Central Railroad Company; Edward B. Adams, of the Mexican Central and the Sonora Railroad Company; Huntington, representing the Southern Pacific; Gould, representing the Missouri Pacific Railroad Company; Henry G. Marquand of the St. Louis & Iron Mountain Railroad Company; John S. Kennedy of the I&GN Railroad Company; J. Henry Work and Frank S. Bond of the Texas & Pacific; and J. B. Horison of the Missouri, Kansas & Texas. General Palmer, C. J. Woerishoffer, representing the Mexican Construction Company, and Thomas Jefferson Coolidge, president of the Atchison, Topeka & Santa Fe, were also invited but were unable to attend.[32]

Although the executives present agreed to work together by forming a committee with General Grant as chairman, no arrangement for harmonizing their interests was reached before this meeting. Gould took advantage of the opportunity to offer his proposal, which in essence called for all parties to have equal rights on all roads built under the agreement and for the parties to refrain from building new lines from those points on the border where lines were already under construction. Gould also proposed that, if they did not approve his proposals, the committee members would then submit their respective claims and differences to General Grant for resolution and accept his decisions. However, no action was taken on Gould's proposals, and the terms of the agreement were deferred.[33]

When the other leaders showed no interest in a cooperative effort in Mexico, Gould moved quickly on his own. First, he acquired the I&GN in December, as previously mentioned, to give him a link across Texas to Laredo on the Mexican border. Although New York had no provision for chartering companies operating in foreign countries, Gould and Grant persuaded the New York legislature to pass one for theirs. Thus on

March 23, 1881, the Mexican Southern Railroad Company was incorporated in New York City with Grant as president, Dodge (a Gould representative) as vice president, and Russell Sage as treasurer. Romero transferred his concession in Oaxaca to the new corporation on March 26, and
two days later he and Grant left for Mexico City to secure a formal concession from the national government with a provision for higher freight
and passenger rates than the Oaxaca government allowed.[34]

GOULD COMES TO GALVESTON

When Gould made his first visit to Galveston on March 7, 1881, and
Grant made his second call on April 1, 1881, the new partners had this
much of their Mexican strategy in place. The *Galveston Daily News* reported that Gould visited briefly in order to inspect his roads and the
southwestern part of the state and to examine the feasibility of establishing a southern steamship line. This line, the *News* learned from reliable
sources, would ply along the Mexican coast to Vera Cruz and other significant points in Mexico, and even down to Central America.[35]

Gould was not on a joyride. With him were all of the top executives of
his far-flung empire, many of whom had been acquired along with the
empire. They included General Thomas T. Eckert, vice president and
general manager of Western Union Telegraph; Samuel Sloan, president of
the Delaware, Lackawanna & Michigan Railroad; Henry G. Marquand,
president of the St. Louis, Iron Mountain, & Southern Railroad; A. A.
Talmadge, general manager of the Missouri Pacific Railroad; Robert S.
Hayes, president of the International & Great Northern Railroad; and
A. L. Hopkins, vice president of Wabash Road.

Gould would rely upon these men in the future to manage his system.
According to Klein, Gould relied heavily upon the advice of key subordinates to guide him, and he in turn treated them well. These men, along
with Herbert M. Hoxie, also from the I&GN, would be the brains behind Gould's Southwestern System—the Missouri Pacific—in the coming decade.[36]

During the two-hour visit, which included a tour of the city and a visit
to the Cotton Exchange, the *News* reporter had difficulty actually talking
with Gould. Once he was introduced to General Eckert as someone
"whom you ought to see." Later, when the reporter asked Gould about the
interview with him that the *New York Herald* had recently published,
Gould told him that it was probably correct, and the *News* carried the
lengthy interview in its coverage of the visit. General Eckert, on his third

visit to Texas, was effusive in his praise for the future of Texas and the Southwest. The moneyed circles in New York, he said, had been focused on the Northwest for some years and now the Southwest was becoming a particularly inviting area for investment.[37]

Gould's own interest in Mexico was brought out in the *Herald* interview. Denying that railroads were overbuilding, he pointed out that his lines would connect with Mexican lines at El Paso and Laredo and that he foresaw an immense foreign market developing in Mexico for American manufactured goods and machinery. He thought that the Mexican mining industry would be given a new impulse because they did not have the new and improved mining machinery available in the United States. He also thought that the Mexican fears of American encroachment would subside as trade grew and its benefits became obvious.[38]

Besides discussing Galveston and its role, Gould also took the opportunity to expound on the nature of corporations and on the proper role of the states in regulating them. It has been suggested that one of Gould's purposes, perhaps his main one, in visiting Texas at this time was to attack pending railroad and telegraph regulation measures coming before the Texas legislature.[39]

Additional light on Gould's activities was provided two weeks later by the Gainesville correspondent to the *News* in a dispatch concerning Gould's desire to connect the Texas & Pacific branch ending at Whitesboro to the main line at Dallas or Fort Worth. T&P officials favored a connection via Denton to Dallas. Gould, it was reported, preferred a route from Gainesville to Cleburne via Denton and Fort Worth, "where a southern extension from the main line will afford a sea-board outlet through a country that will support a good local traffic." The article went on to point out that the line from Gainesville to Belton and on to Galveston was "the golden belt of Texas," according to county assessments published by the *News*. The plan envisioned a connection with the Gulf, Colorado & Santa Fe, building north, somewhere between Belton and Cleburne, thus forming the seaboard connection to the Gulf of Mexico.[40]

Arriving in Galveston on April 1, Grant and Romero proceeded again to the Tremont House hotel where the *News* correspondent obtained a thirty-minute interview. Not surprisingly, Romero, now president of a Mexican railroad, was well into the "selling of Mexico," in contrast to the purely ceremonial nature of his earlier visit to Galveston. Grant thought that Mexicans no longer feared American intrusion and welcomed American capital; that large sugar, coffee, and wheat plantations being devel-

oped would provide for a two-way trade; and that the economic development of the country would bring political stability. He ended the interview
by expressing the opinion that a reciprocity treaty would equally enhance
the interests of both countries. His only comment on Galveston was a reference to the necessity of deep water to attract the railroads, lest, in spite
of Galveston's geographical advantages, they seek other ports.[41]

Grant and Romero went on to Mexico, where the greeting was not
quite as enthusiastic as before. Grant was now the president of a railroad
and Romero had political enemies. There was considerable rumor and
speculation about Grant's activities, and the fears of American encroachment were not completely dead. Grant responded to the accusations with
many of the same remarks that he made in the Galveston interview: that
trade between the two countries could be mutually beneficial and that
Americans were not interested in further expansion of their nation's borders.[42] Gould proceeded with his plans for Mexico by obtaining a concession for a line through eastern Mexico from Laredo through Ciudad Vic-
toria to Mexico City, with branches to Tampico and Vera Cruz. This line
was named the Mexican Oriental, Interoceanic & International Railroad
Company.[43]

With Gould and Grant now joining the efforts under way by the
Mexican Central (affiliated with but not owned by the Atchison, Topeka
& Santa Fe) and the Mexican National (affiliated with General William J.
Palmer's Denver & Rio Grande), the pace of events began to heat up. In
an editorial entitled, "The Race for Mexico," the *Galveston Daily News*
declared that "considerable advantage will be obtained . . . by the line from
the United States first connecting with the Mexican system." The *News*
was describing the contest between the Boston capitalists who controlled
the AT&SF and Gould, both of whom were building toward Mexican
connections. The AT&SF was extending its Albuquerque-Deming, New
Mexico, line to El Paso, and Gould was extending the I&GN to Laredo.[44]
A similar article in the *New York Times* describing the railroad activity in
Mexico stated that the roads were the necessary instrumentality of Mexico's industrial and commercial growth and that the country was without
the means to build them.[45] The *News* also obtained an eyewitness ap-
praisal of the prospects for Mexican trade from Galveston merchant Marx
Marx [*sic*], described as a "shrewd, far-seeing and enterprising businessman, whose ideas are not formed hastily, but are based upon close and actual observation." He reported that there was a ready market for Texas
cotton and other American products and that Galveston would soon have
railroad connections with Mexico City. He also cited the need for the Vera

Cruz steamship connection that Gould had expressed interest in during his March 3 visit.[46]

On a broader scale, Warner P. Sutton, who served as commercial agent, consul, and general consul first at Matamoros, near the mouth of the Rio Grande, and later upstream at Laredo, did much to promote and facilitate the development of Mexican trade with the voluminous reports and statistics he submitted to Washington while at these posts between 1878 and 1893.[47] The reports received national attention, as indicated in the following excerpt from an article in the *American Mail and Export Journal:* "As far as Mexico is concerned, our consuls seem to be fully alive to the present opportunities for the cultivation of commercial relations with Mexico, and our Department of State gives prominence, as it should do, to all reports from that country. It only remains for our merchants and manufacturers to study the markets thoroughly, and then follow up their advantages, not uneasily or hungrily, but judiciously and generously, so that the profits which will accrue to Mexico shall be equal to the profits which shall accrue to the United States."[48]

The *Export Journal* also projected in the most glowing terms the future benefits to be derived from the development of the railroads and the subsequent increase in commerce:

> Mexico at present is full of armed Americans—armed with the implements of commerce and science—and the Mexicans receive them with open arms. In a little while the railroad and the steamship will bring the products of Mexico to our markets daily and return with the products and manufactures which she may require and which we can and will supply. Within the next few years the City of Mexico and the great marts of the United States will be within "hailing distance," so to speak, and the peoples of the two republics shall be as homogeneous, commercially and socially speaking, as the citizens of any two of the States of our own Union.[49]

Sutton's reporting doubtlessly encouraged investors and merchants to begin looking south of the border for opportunity. He would continue reporting as the Mexican Central and Mexican National railroads were completed and the hoped-for benefits began to accrue. Whereas British and German merchants had dominated Mexican trade through Vera Cruz, much of that trade now began turning northward. Mexico began selling more of her exports to the United States, and her people acquired tastes for varied imports. American investment increased, and foods supplies could be moved southward when drought and famine threatened. Later

Mexican economists would question the impact of these railroads, but initially, during Sutton's tour of duty, the results were favorable.[50]

CREATING THE MISSOURI PACIFIC

While Gould's plans for the extensions into Mexico were developing rapidly and favorably in 1881, he was also moving in a similar fashion toward the creation of his Southwestern System in the United States. In April, Thomas A. Scott, having failed in his attempt to obtain a federal subsidy to extend the Texas & Pacific to El Paso, and now an invalid, sold his holdings to Gould. Suddenly rumors were flying about his plans to consolidate all of the roads into a single southwestern company. By an exchange of stock, the Katy, already leased to the Missouri Pacific, absorbed the International, or I&GN. Next, Gould attempted to consolidate the Texas & Pacific with the Iron Mountain and, failing, merged the Iron Mountain with the Missouri Pacific and had the Texas & Pacific absorb the New Orleans Pacific, the connection from Shreveport to New Orleans and the Gulf of Mexico. The impact of these moves on Wall Street was tremendous, and all of Gould's stocks soared: the Missouri Pacific from 85 to 110; the Texas & Pacific from 41 to 73; the Iron Mountain from 52 to 86; the I&GN from 50 to 92; and the Katy from 40 to 50.[51]

In addition to these moves, which touched most of the populated area of the state at the time, Gould also acquired the GH&H, Galveston's tie to Houston. A rumor of the sale was reported on May 22, 1881, and was confirmed two days later.[52] The people of Galveston may have anticipated this event after N. A. Cowdrey of New York, the trustee for the bankrupt GH&H, met with Colonel Moody, Runge, and members of the Cotton Exchange. Although he is not reported as having mentioned the railroad specifically, he did inform the members "that it was the duty of leading citizens to put themselves in communications with parties looking at this city as an eventual great position in the distribution of the world's commerce, notably Jay Gould . . . if his interests could be directed toward Galveston, it would be to the advantage of the city. Times were fast changing and men should change with them." The reference to "change" apparently referred to the rejection of overtures made by General Grenville Dodge, on behalf of Gould, to purchase a share of the GC&SF during Dodge's visit in December, 1879. Cowdrey also visited with Judge John Darragh, president of the Wharf Company, and toured the docks, so terminal facilities were likewise a subject of discussion.[53]

Confirmation of the rumors of May 24 came from several sources, including the general manager of the GH&H. He received a letter from Cowdrey, advising him of Cowdrey's sale of his interest to Gould and Sage.[54] The line would be leased to the I&GN, which in turn was under the control of Missouri Pacific, giving Gould his outlet to the Gulf of Mexico. Having achieved this goal, Gould could now turn to the extension of the T&P across Texas. As Gould immersed himself in battles in the Midwest with his other foes, the Union Pacific appeared to be the center of his Southwestern System, especially after he organized a syndicate to build an extension to San Francisco. He broke an 1880 agreement that the Union Pacific—not he—had signed, and threatened to build the Missouri Pacific through Burlington territory to Omaha. These moves, which attracted both attention and controversy, diverted attention from Texas, the real battlefield.[55]

GOULD EYES GALVESTON AND THE GC&SF

The war between the Gulf, Colorado & Santa Fe and the Jay Gould interests began late in December, 1880, when General Grenville Dodge, Gould's right-hand man in Texas, came to Galveston, along with Robert S. Hayes, president of the International & Great Northern. Gould's interest in Galveston was well-known by this time, and it was only natural that rumors persisted regarding the reason for General Dodge's presence. One was that he was seeking an agreement with the GC&SF management whereby the Missouri Pacific could use the GC&SF tracks from Belton to Fort Worth, thus making it unnecessary to build two lines. A second, more intriguing rumor was that Gould wished to purchase a sufficient amount of stock in the GC&SF to have a voice in the management of its affairs. As usual, General Dodge was willing to discuss publicly a number of subjects but not the matter of prime interest. GC&SF president George Sealy likewise had no comment.[1]

The speculation surrounding the visitors was intensified when N. A. Cowdrey of New York, the trustee for the GH&H who was also in the city, stated that Gould was planning to visit Galveston at an early date and was impressed with the idea of making the mouth of the Brazos River a terminal. Cowdrey was very blunt in his remarks regarding the inadequacy of facilities at the port, causing the *Galveston Daily News* to comment editorially that "old time ideas of chartered privileges upon commerce will have to give way in a great measure before this modern financial power."[2]

Both President Sealy and his brother John, the GC&SF general manager, continued to refrain from commenting upon the rumors, in spite of the *News* assertions that it had confirmed its information on the issues at hand. General Dodge wrote to Gould on December 28, 1880, giving him the facts that he had gathered on the state of the GC&SF and indicating that he would make a cash offer for the stock after a trip to New Orleans.[3]

On January, 14, 1881, he again wrote to Gould: "I cannot do much with Galveston and the Santa Fe people on the exchange of stock. We can buy the road so it would cost us about $17,000 per mile of completed and equipped road." He also told Gould of encountering rain, snow, and sleet in Texas and suggested that he wait until spring for his trip.[4] On the next day, the *News's* New York dispatch divulged the following information: "It is reported on good authority that Jay Gould will build to the mouth of the Brazos on his own responsibility, if others do not choose to join him."[5] Intimidation and threats were among the tools of the railroad barons in those days, and apparently the GC&SF directors and stockholders were being introduced to them. On the following day, January 16, 1881, the *News* reported "that the ultimatum of Jay Gould with respect to the acquisition of a controlling interest in the Gulf, Colorado and Santa Fe railroad was wired yesterday to an officer of that company accompanied by threatened aggressive measures on the part of Mr. Gould should the Santa Fe management be contumacious and decline to surrender on the terms proposed."[6]

On January 20, 1881, General Dodge informed Gould that he and Sealy had reached an agreement of terms of a sale that Sealy was in the process of presenting to his stockholders for approval. General Dodge seemed confident in this letter to Gould and suggested that Sealy be kept on the board of directors and that Gould add Robert S. Hayes and Herbert M. Hoxie.[7]

Approval was not immediately forthcoming, and Dodge advised Gould on January 25, 1881: "If the New York or Galveston stockholders of the Santa Fe road approach you, give them no satisfaction. Make them come to my terms."[8] Two days later in another letter to Gould, Dodge indicated that he was still waiting for approval and asked Gould to keep the sale private until the Galveston people agreed.[9]

The sale to Gould was never completed. Since a copy of the agreement has not survived, the facts are not available. Since Sealy and Dodge had gone so far as to complete a memorandum of agreement, it appears that Sealy may had been at odds with the majority of his directors or stockholders. The minutes of the board of directors meetings of January 10, February 14, and March 14, 1881, contain no mention of resolutions proposing the sale. However, in order to maintain secrecy, Sealy may have resorted to informal polling of the board.[10]

GOULD PURSUES THE GC&SF

Whatever the circumstances of January, 1881, everything was pleasant and cordial when Gould made his first visit to Galveston on March 7, 1881.

Traveling by a special train composed of the president's coaches of the St. Louis, Iron Mountain & Southern and Missouri Pacific roads plus a baggage car, the Gould party arrived shortly after lunch on the seventh. Since all of the public conveyances had been commandeered for electioneering purposes, the party first walked to the Western Union offices. From there they proceeded to the Cotton Exchange, where they were met by a large gathering of the Exchange board and other business leaders. Gould was accompanied by all of his top executives, a very impressive group. Commenting upon Gould himself, his small stature, and his quiet voice, a *News* reporter observed that "had it not been known that he actually was Jay Gould, he would have been the least conspicuous and least noticed of the visitors."[11]

The visit was brief, and the party left the island at around 3 P.M. Nevertheless, the real point of the visit was clear. Gould himself was reticent; the major part of the *News* coverage consisted of the reprint of a lengthy interview from the *New York Herald*. But an unidentified informant repeated the threat reported in December that unless "the people of Galveston will give him the right encouragement and manifest the proper feeling toward him, Gould would make the mouth of the Brazos his Gulf port." This time, however, Gould offered the carrot as well as the stick. It was announced that he was contemplating a steamship line to Mexico and South America, implying that there was much more at stake for Galveston than the railroad connection and terminal facilities. But, as the reporter prepared to ask the critical question—what kind of encouragement did the great railroader want?—Hayes announced that it was time for the party to move on.[12]

Whether or not the sale of the GC&SF was mandatory to satisfy Gould remained an unanswered question. The months following the Gould visit were rife with rumor and speculation. Some of the continuing speculations pertained to the plan for the steamship line. The remainder focused on the persistent rumors surrounding the GC&SF. Shortly after Gould left it was revealed "that he had made the proposition to the people of that city that if they would subscribe $100,000 he would duplicate the sum for the establishment of a daily line of steamers," the interest being offered for the sole purpose of securing activity on the part of the people of Galveston in behalf of the successful operation of the line.[13] Colonel J. M. Eddy, general superintendent of construction for the Missouri Pacific, visited Galveston on March 28, 1881, to negotiate for the sale of fourteen blocks of ground on the bay front. In an interview, Colonel Eddy stated, "I don't think the people of Galveston should let us pay too much for the grounds that we need." Again the possibility of building at the Brazos was raised, and Eddy discussed his plans to inspect the area.[14] At the same time he tried to make the scope of the opportunity being offered very clear: "We will, from the outset, bring into and take out of Galveston more freights than both your roads now do combined. Here we will be a direct connection of, and seaboard terminus for a system ranging through this state, reaching to St. Louis, Chicago, Colorado, and the Pacific slope, and of course will haul to this point thousands of tons of freight that does not come this way at all. We want track room for at least 1000 cars."[15]

The other set of speculations pertained to the continuing moves of Gould toward the GC&SF. Gould officials talked about Missouri Pacific lines into Galveston from both Fort Worth and Laredo. So while it was understood that the Gould organization had the resources to do whatever it desired, there were those who suspected they were bluffing in order to get control of both the GC&SF and the Galveston, Houston & Henderson. A dispatch from Austin to the *News* quoted a Gould official as saying that George Sealy had agreed to a joint arrangement between the two roads that would make Galveston the Gulf terminus of the Missouri Pacific, and give the GC&SF access to St. Louis over Missouri Pacific lines. But again the GC&SF Board of Directors had not approved the agreement. Minutes of the board meetings do not show any action taken on this proposition.[16]

But a week later the *News* was reporting a willingness on the part of representatives of the GC&SF "to divide the loaf" with Gould.[17] Rumors persisted for the next two weeks, and the *Railway Gazette* carried a story that Gould had actually secured half interest in the GC&SF.[18] The air was cleared somewhat when Sealy finally granted an interview on April 19, 1881. He stated that propositions for all or half of the road had been "sometime ago rejected by the directory, since which time no proposition had been considered or is pending for consideration." Sealy also said that the had no positive news about the Missouri Pacific coming to Galveston but that he did not see direct competition between the lines, as the two roads would be some distance apart with water courses between them. He added that the price of certain wharf and depot grounds had been provided to Gould by the Galveston City Company, but there had been no reply. In response to a question pertaining to the sale of $1,000,000 of GC&SF bonds, which had provoked rumors of the Gould purchase, Sealy commented that this sale by him for private accounts did not involve either Gould or the GC&SF.[19]

On April 29, 1881, the *Railway Gazette* quoted the chief engineer of the Missouri, Kansas & Texas as stating that it was an established fact that the road would build from Fort Worth to Galveston. Whether Gould was bluffing or not—and it appears that he was not—negotiations for both the terminal facilities and part ownership in the GC&SF came to a halt. Just as the parties were closemouthed about the negotiations while they were in progress, they were silent regarding any animosity that may have been felt because a deal was not reached. From the hostile activities that occurred over the next five years, which will be discussed, it can be inferred that the Gould forces were not happy with their inability to achieve their goals.

Sealy was equally silent about this problem with his own board of directors, who apparently voted him down twice on Gould proposals that he had accepted. As previously mentioned, these votes do not appear in the board minutes of those months; consequently there is no evidence regarding a split in the board. Sealy himself had no comments to make regarding these rejections, and none of the board members spoke out to defend his actions or to attack the Gould people. Since the proposals offered the railroad connections to the north and west that the Galveston was seeking, one has to assume that the fear of being overwhelmed by the power and wealth of Jay Gould caused the opposition.

THE *DAILY NEWS* SUPPORTS GOULD

Colonel Alfred H. Belo and the *News* were not merely reporters during this process. In an editorial entitled "Encourage the Gould Syndicate," the *News,* after reviewing the Gould strategy, pointed out that:

The vastness of Mr. Gould's transportation schemes begins to break upon the comprehension. This all means for Galveston a magnificent commercial future. A trade inaugurated under such auspices would grow of its own volume. There are points in the consummation of this project, however, that parties with interest in Galveston will be required to aid and assist. Will he be met in a progressive and liberal spirit? Although Mr. Gould is not seeking an outlet in the role of a beggarly mendicant, he is not the man to stand any superabundance of nonsense in an opposite direction. It will be to the interest of Galveston to encourage the Gould syndicate.[20]

In a similar editorial only the day before, the *News* had been even more emphatic in its conclusion: "Mr. Jay Gould had better be give a pretty solid show. The City of Galveston never had a brighter period in her existence than now, and this bright period it will not do to cloud with the shadow of an old-time barnacle policy."[21] As the next month passed without any negotiations completed with Gould, Colonel Belo was restrained in his comments, but the *News* did carry an editorial from the *Houston Post* that was very blunt and pointed in its criticism:

> **Hence, we are of the opinion that the directors of the Santa Fe road did a very unwise thing when they refused to sell to a controlling interest in their road. Such a policy inclines us to believe that the monopoly that controls the Galveston interests does not, at the bottom, desire to secure the early and pronounced expansion of business and trade in their city. It would militate against their own plans, and would disturb, if not break up forever the completeness of their own power over business affairs in Galveston. They have prospered and grown rich under the old and slow ways.**[22]

Similar criticism of narrow interests in Galveston satisfied with the status quo and opposed to change would be heard again. But at this time there was ample reason to fear turning the destiny of one's city over completely to Jay Gould. So Gould virtually disappeared from the newspaper columns, and George Sealy turned his efforts toward surviving in a situation where Gould, now his enemy, would soon control all of the competing railroads in Texas (the MKT, the I&GN, and the GH&H running north and south) as well as the connecting roads (the Texas & Pacific and the Iron Mountain).

SEALY'S DEFENSIVE MEASURES

No sooner had the Gould affair began to die down than stories began to circulate regarding Sealy's first move to cope with the new situation. One report suggested that the GC&SF would extend its line northeastward from Fort Worth through Denton, Collin, and Lamar Counties to Paris and a connection with the St. Louis & San Francisco Railroad (the Frisco) on the Red River. This announcement was followed shortly by the news that officials of the GC&SF had met with officials of the Chicago, Texas & Mexican Central Railway Company who were planning to build a Cleburne-Paris section of their road. The acquisition of this section would provide the GC&SF its connection to the Frisco, which would parallel Gould's MKT to St. Louis. On June 8, 1881, it was announced that an agreement had been reached, with the GC&SF providing access to the Gulf in return for access to St. Louis and Chicago.[23] With an eastern outlet around the Gould lines assured, the *News* saw unlimited opportunities for Galveston after the GC&SF reached Santa Fe, and the Chicago, Texas & Mexican Central reached the Rio Grande River and crossed Mexico to

Topolobampo on the Pacific coast.[24] The *St. Louis Register*, as quoted by
the *News*, was equally enthralled by the developments and spoke highly of
the GC&SF accomplishments. Of course, its emphasis was upon the benefits to St. Louis merchants, but that was seen by the short-sighted *News*
not to "prejudice the interests of the Island City."[25]

The GC&SF eventually took control of the Chicago, Texas & Mexican
Central on July 1, 1882, receiving the 52 miles from Cleburne to Dallas,
with the connection to Paris still to be accomplished. Although it did not
attract a lot of comment at the time, both the *News* and the *Railway
Gazette* carried small notices in April, 1882, that Sealy might be thinking of other connections for the GS&SF. The reports stated that a survey
had been undertaken by the Atchison, Topeka & Santa Fe to determine
the most feasible route from Caldwell, Kansas, through the Indian
Territory to a connection with the GC&SF. In view of the fact that it eventually would be these two railways that would consolidate, the news was
of more significance than the one inch of space that it received. The survey suggests that Sealy may have been quietly negotiating with the AT&SF
for four years.[26] J. L. Truslow and W. H. Holabird, Texas agents of the
AT&SF, were in Galveston in January and apparently were more than
tourists.[27]

The moves for connections with the Frisco and the Atchison were fol-
lowed immediately by the announcement of a traffic agreement with the
Texas & St. Louis. Open warfare between the Gould system and the
Texas & St. Louis, the Cotton Belt, had begun in July, 1881, when it be-
gan extending its line from Texarkana to St. Louis, paralleling Gould's
Iron Mountain. The new alliance would give the GC&SF access to Waco,
Corsicana, Athens, Tyler, Pittsburg, and Texarkana as well as a route to
St. Louis that Gould did not control.[28]

President Sealy's next move may be considered even more ambitious.
The *Railway Gazette* reported that Sealy, Frank P. Killeen, GC&SF
secretary and assistant general manager, and Waters Davis, a director, con-
ferred with officials of both the Chicago & Alton and the Chicago,
Burlington & Quincy regarding a scheme for extending the system to
Chicago. The proposal was as follows: "That the Gulf, Colorado and
Santa Fe will extend its line from Fort Worth to the southern boundary of
the Indian Territory; that the Chicago & Alton (or Burlington) shall extend its line from Kansas City to the northern boundary of the Indian
Territory; and that the two interests shall then join in a new company and
build the intermediate section of road across Indian Territory. . . . By way
of inducement to join in this combination, the Gulf, Colorado and Santa
Fe will guarantee its northern ally and connection 400,000 bales of cotton
annually, besides the bulk of the cattle trade of Western Texas."[29]

Neither company, however, was inclined to accept the proposition or enter into negotiations for different terms. The *Daily News* even seemed to be surprised about the feature of the proposal guaranteeing 400,000 bales of cotton annually to the northern connection. Obviously this implied that less cotton might be coming to the port of Galveston. But, by 1879, it was becoming obvious that the penetration of northern and central Texas by rail connections to St. Louis was having a major impact upon the movement of cotton to such an extent that Dallas was becoming a major cotton market and transcontinental rail would gradually supplant coast-wise shipping. The initial announcement of these terms was followed three days later by a statement that this offer was not denied by the GC&SF.[30]

Following their conversations in Chicago, T. J. Potter, third vice president of the Burlington, provided a letter of introduction for Sealy and Killeen to A. E. Touzalin, the first vice president in Boston, as they planned to continue their trip to New York and Boston.[31] Sealy returned to Galveston from New York June 5 and granted a brief interview, but he was as tight-lipped as usual regarding the reported events. He had only engaged in some friendly discussions of railroad matters, and no direct propositions had been made by either party.[32]

Concurrent with Sealy's strategic moves aimed at alliances with other lines that would strengthen the GC&SF's position, other officials were involved in the lower-level tactical moves against the Gould system. In May representatives of all the Texas railroads, including Herbert M. Hoxie, general manager of the Gould Southwestern roads; Colonel Thomas W. Peirce, president of the Galveston, Harrisburg & San Antonio; John Sealy, general manager of the GC&SF; and Oscar G. Murray, general freight and passenger agent for the GC&SF, met in Galveston to establish a pooling arrangement. The following day a Houston dispatch to the *News* revealed that the Galveston meeting was a follow-up to a previously held meeting in New Orleans at which all of the roads except the GH&SA and the GC&SF agreed to a pool "on the basis of 50 and 50."[33] The Galveston meeting was held for the purpose of persuading the holdouts to join, but no progress was made. When offered the 50-50 proposition, GC&SF officials pointed out that they were now getting 75 percent of the business out of Galveston and 90 percent from many points on the line. The meeting adjourned with a rate war expected to follow.[34]

Quickly the *Galveston Daily News* was inspired to speculate upon the order of battle of the opposing forces in the coming war and its significance to Galveston:

In the event that the vapors of rumors should clear away and reveal the palpable fact of such a condition of affairs as hinted at, it would become an interesting study to see how the lines of coalition would run and what forces would be marshaled by the respective combinations. Perhaps one step in the formation of the lines for aggression or defense was taken in the passenger and traffic agreement between the Gulf, Colorado & Santa Fe and the Texas & St. Louis Narrow Gauge roads. . . . In the development of the conflict, if really impending, it is supposed that the Gould and Morgan interests upon the one side will be arrayed against the Huntington, Gulf, Colorado & Santa Fe, and the combined narrow gauge interests on the other. With such forces arrayed against each other, results of the greatest importance to Galveston would be involved, because the point in issue would be nothing less that the control of Texas trade to the deep sea.[35]

Evidence of a warming up of the hostilities was soon to appear. Interviewed by the *News*, an unidentified but prominent Gould official pointed out, "We did have a contract with them [GC&SF], which expired on the 15th of March, since which time they have been put . . . on the same basis with other roads with which working arrangements do not exist." Soon rumors were heard in New York that Gould was bring the Houston & Texas Central into the battle against the GC&SF,[36] and those rumors were shortly confirmed when the H&TC refused rights to the GC&SF entering Dallas, causing the GC&SF to seek its own right-of-way and to build an additional two miles of track.[37]

On July 18, 1882, the GC&SF agreement with the Texas & St. Louis narrow gauge began to take effect. Colonel J. B. Vandyne, the Cotton Belt's general superintendent, took a party of guests from Waco to McGregor, the junction with the GC&SF. The road would continue west 20 miles to Gatesville, making a total of 456 miles from its starting place at Pine Bluff, Arkansas.[38] The GC&SF soon announced that its surveying corps had laid out a route through Dallas from the depot site of the Chicago, Texas & Mexican Central to Harwood Street, then north to another junction with the Cotton Belt. Thus the GC&SF completed this very important step in establishing an eastern connection that would free itself from Gould control.[39]

On the same day that the *News*'s Dallas dispatch was announcing the connection there, the Washington correspondent was reporting news of broader significance, the passage of the Act granting right-of-way to the Frisco through the Indian Territory, establishing the right of eminent domain there as well as in all other territories. The bill granted the Frisco the right to build from Fort Smith through the Choctaw Nation toward the Red River and Paris. The act required that a map of the route be filed in one year and that the road be completed in two years. By that time both the GC&SF and the H&TC would probably have extended their lines to Paris, and the Frisco would also have completed its track from Van Buren to St. Louis.[40] Even better news was that, contrary to earlier rumors, it turned out to be Huntington who had purchased a controlling interest in the Frisco rather than Gould, who had only four of the thirteen directors, and that the Frisco was now looked upon as a competing road to the Gould lines to St. Louis—the MKT from Denison and the Iron Mountain from Texarkana.[41]

Unlike the cotton crop across the South in 1882, the crop in Texas was up and all of the Texas roads were benefiting that season. In spite of the difficulties with the Gould lines, the GC&SF in the month of September, for example, earned $194,653, compared with $120,196 for the same month in the previous year.[42] By the end of the year, the *News* was reporting considerable inquiry in financial circles for securities, leading to the conclusion that "the increased earnings of the Galveston enterprise must necessarily tend to enhance the value of its securities. The Gulf, Colorado and Santa Fe is doubtless regarded as a valuable and desirable property in intelligent railroad circles."[43]

As 1883 opened the GC&SF continued its expansion until it totaled 523 miles: 273 miles on the Main line to Lampasas, 127 miles on the Fort Worth branch, 42 miles on the Eastern branch to Montgomery County, 55 miles on the Dallas branch, and 24 miles on the Houston branch. The road listed the value of its rolling stock at $722,650, based upon 41 locomotives, 19 passenger cars, 683 boxcars, 540 flatcars, and other miscellaneous equipment.[44]

By April, 1883, the full impact of Gould's consolidation of his Southwestern System was being felt in Galveston. On the first of April it was announced that the Missouri Pacific, the name for the system, would now run three fast express trains between Galveston and St. Louis with Pullman palace sleeping cars available. The system included the GH&H to Houston; the I&GN to Mineola; the MKT from Denison to St. Louis; and the Texas & Pacific and Iron Mountain roads from Mineola through Texarkana to St. Louis. The advertisement showed the times for the connecting trains on to Chicago and New York.[45]

Without any advance fanfare, Gould and his traveling party visited Galveston again on May 4, 1883. In its May 3 edition, the *Daily News* printed an editorial discussing the problems between the GC&SF and the Gould roads, quoting the *St. Louis Globe-Democrat* as recently blaming the problems on the GC&SF's failure to stand by agreements. It also reported having private information from New York that friends of the road there blamed the problems on the local management. Referring to the need for connections, the editorial again mentioned the Atchison, Topeka & Santa Fe as a possibility. The mention of the AT&SF suggests that the *Daily News* may have known of secret negotiations under way, or may even have been conveying "planted" news to the visitors on the way. The May 4 edition carried one of the few substantive interviews given by John Sealy, the GC&SF general manager. In it he released an exchange of letters between himself and H. M. Hoxie, the Missouri Pacific third vice president. On April 14, Hoxie had notified John Sealy that "we respectively decline, after the first day of May, 1883, to honor your tickets or baggage checks, issued over any of our lines."[46]

GOULD RETURNS TO GALVESTON

In his reply Sealy offered: "I consider such action not only a great injustice, but a discrimination against this company made apparently with a view of injuring and harassing its business." Sealy went on to deny departing from established rates and accused the Missouri Pacific of giving other competitors preferential treatment and of preventing other lines from selling tickets over the GC&SF. Despite the obvious problems, everything was cordial and gracious when Gould, again accompanied by Sloan, Hayes, Talmadge, Hoxie, and a host of others, arrived at 11:30 A.M. the same day and were met at the depot by W. H. Harding, the GH&H president. The party drove through the city in carriages and visited the Cotton Exchange, where a brief reception was held and Captain Charles Vidor introduced the gentlemen and extended courtesies to them. Gould was highly pleased with the appearance of the city and was very interested in Major Mansfield's latest comments on the prospects of the Army Engineers achieving a depth of eighteen feet over the bar by fall. While Gould and others were driven around the city, Hayes and Hoxie made a call upon John Sealy. The meeting was social in nature, and Hoxie met a lot of his old friends. Undoubtedly, business matters were discussed, but, in the custom of the day, no information was provided to the press.[47]

Unlike during his previous visit, Gould did grant the *Daily News* reporter an extended interview on the way from Houston to Galveston. He talked freely about railroad matters in general in Texas and about his own plans, including the extensions into Mexico. He spoke emphatically about the importance of the deep water harbor to the railroads and of the importance of the citizens of Galveston taking hold of this matter and seeing to it that a channel of sufficient depth was secured. He repeated the possibility of a steamship line to Vera Cruz operating from Galveston.

The cordiality continued after the Gould train left for Rosenberg over the GC&SF tracks. A Gould representative said there was no foundation for the St. Louis report blaming the GC&SF for breaking agreements and that friends of the GC&SF in New York were mistaken in blaming problems on the local management of the road. The *Daily News* concluded its reporting on the visit with the statement that "it is an incontrovertible fact that he [Gould] has done and is doing for Texas a wonderful amount of work in forcing the State to a front rank in the Union."[48]

Gould departed, saying that his party would go to Laredo and perhaps to Monterrey, and then to San Antonio. He made no mention in Galveston of meeting with General Porfirio Diaz, the ex-president of Mexico. However, the *New York Times* reported that Diaz met the Gould train in Austin on March 7, 1883. Apparently the "selling of Mexico" was still in full swing as Diaz continued to New York City where he was hosted at large dinners by General Grant and later by Collis P. Huntington. General Diaz, president of Mexico from 1876 to 1880, was out of office as this time, but he would return to a dictatorial presidency and remain there until overthrown by Francisco Madero in the revolution of 1910. During Diaz's reign (called the "Porfiriato" in Mexico), the railroads expanded from 287 miles to a complete grid of almost 12,000 miles.[49]

The Gould party had no sooner left the state than the subject of connection with the AT&SF arose again. Commenting on reports from Boston of an imminent construction war between the AT&SF and the Gould lines in Kansas, the *Daily News* virtually advocated the GC&SF preparing for a "hand in the row." It described the opportunity thus: "The Gulf, Colorado and Santa Fe would hold an invincible position were it once in direct connection with the railway system concentrating at Kansas City, and going in there backed by as powerful a syndicate at that of the Atchison, Topeka and Santa Fe, it would carry a weight with it which would readily decide conventional issues."[50]

Whatever may have been transpiring privately, nothing was said publicly about any negotiations with the AT&SF at this time. Rumors continued to fly about involving the AT&SF and now the Fort Worth & Denver City, a road extending from Fort Worth northwest to Wichita Falls. The FW&DC was mentioned by the *Daily News* in conjunction with another rumor that about thirty-five Galveston GC&SF stockholders controlling a majority of the $4,500,000 worth of outstanding stock had pooled their interests to vote against any sale of the road. President George Sealy, more informative that usual, revealed in an interview a week later that, in support of the rumor, the Galveston stockholders placed a majority of the stock in a strongbox under lock and key where it would remain indefinitely. He went on to point out that the Galveston investors, being men of means who had put only a portion of their surplus into the road, could hold their stock indefinitely without dividends, and would be compelled neither to sell it nor borrow money upon it. Asked by the interviewer to account for the presence of such surplus of wealth in Galveston, Sealy explained that the great secret was that the merchants of Galveston were men who came to stay. Unlike other southern merchants who made their money and moved north, the men of Galveston had stayed and invested their money in Galveston and Texas.[51]

With the outlook still favorable for its future prospects, the stockholders of the GC&SF voted to approve second mortgage bonds for additional construction on August 1, 1883, and also passed the following resolution: "That it is the opinion of this Board that it is advisable for the Company to secure the right of way through the Indian Territory running north from a point on the Red River, west of Denison, and that the Executive Committee be authorized to secure the same."[52]

Implementation of this resolution occurred December 1, 1883, when the *Daily News* announced that Senator Richard Coke would introduce the "Santa Fe Bill" in the next session of Congress to provide a right-of-way from the Red River to the Kansas Border, west of Coffeyville. At this point the GC&SF would be within 50 miles of a connection with either the AT&SF, the Burlington, or the Alton.[53]

As 1883 drew to a close, President Sealy and his board of directors found themselves having survived a third year of hostile relationships and obstructive tactics from the Gould system. In fact, it was more than survival. Statistics from the *New York Financial Chronicle,* as reported in the *Daily News,* showed earnings up for the GC&SF in both September and October over those same months in 1882.[54] It seemed that Gould could do nothing to strangle the GC&SF, and with the stockholders agreement to hold their stock, he could not buy it. The GC&SF was continuing to prosper and grow in value, and at least the AT&SF was interested in some kind of joint arrangement, merger, or purchase.

RIGHT-OF-WAY IN THE INDIAN TERRITORY

When the *Railroad Gazette* announced in its August 8, 1884, edition the conclusion of a traffic agreement between the GC&SF and the Missouri Pacific, it in effect meant that the three-and-a-half-year war against the

Gould system was over. In reporting the announcement, the *Gazette* said: "Negotiations for this agreement have been conducted very quietly, but it looks very much as the Missouri Pacific Co. had finally come to terms and agreed to grant what the Gulf, Colorado and Santa Fe wished, rather than to see another line in the Indian Territory parallel to the Missouri, Kansas and Texas."[55]

Details of the agreement were not provided, but under the agreement through business would be exchanged and there would be an understanding as to the maintenance of rates to and from Texas points. The arrangements took effect on August 1, 1884, and necessary changes in schedules to provide for close connections were to be made as soon as possible. The GC&SF immediately published changes to improve connections with the Missouri Pacific for travel to the north and east.[56]

The final stroke for the Gould forces may have been the passage by Congress of the bill giving the GC&SF its right-of-way through the Indian Territory to the Kansas border. The bill opened the door for the GC&SF to start building immediately toward one of its potential connections, parallel with although not close to the MKT route from Denison to southeastern Kansas. The bill had been introduced as planned in January by Senator Coke, and Walter Gresham, attorney for the GC&SF, went to Washington to manage it through Congress. Gresham's first act in his management of the bill was to have it stand alone instead combining it with the similar bill being proposed for the right-of-way of the AT&SF and its subsidiary, the Southern Kansas. The bill was meeting opposition from both Indians and members of Congress, and it was reported that Gresham was yielding point after point to meet objections.[57]

When the bill came up in the regular order for a Senate vote on March 4, Senator Benjamin Harrison of Indiana, who had been delaying the bill continuously, again objected, at the behest of Senator John J. Ingalls of Kansas, the sponsor of the AT&SF bill, who apparently wanted the two bills considered at the same time. In the meantime, the number of bills for right-of-way had grown to five, then seven; and the Senate was faced with a protest from the principal chief of the Cherokee and Creek Nation, Dennis W. Bushyhead.[58]

The attempt to seek the GC&SF right-of-way took place against a background of twenty years of the white man's encroachment on the Indian Territory. The Treaties of 1866 had established the status of the Five Civilized Tribes and the Indian Territory for the post-Civil War period, and these treaties required the Indians to consent to the building of railroads. The first chartered, on July 27, 1866, was an outgrowth of the route surveys authorized by Congress back in 1853. In 1868 General

William J. Palmer, who had been engaged in surveys, published his report showing a proposed route for the Atlantic and Pacific across the Cherokee Nation and the Indian Territory to Albuquerque, with a branch, the Kansas City, Fort Scott & Gulf, running south to Galveston. The second was the Missouri, Kansas & Texas, which followed the old Texas Road, or Fort Gibson Trail, a famous cattle trail as well as a wagon route for immigrants, merchants, and armies.[59]

By 1884, the territory was threatened with, in addition to encroaching railroads, ever increasing numbers of white settlers and the large cattle drives over the various trails across the territory. The combined effects of exaggerated accounts of the quality of the land and exaggerated hopes of the territory being opened to settlement brought a large number of "boomers" both into the territory and to its borders. Although the land rush of April 22, 1889, to the Unassigned Lands, "Oklahoma," was still five years away, the threat to their sovereignty was becoming obvious to the Indian leaders.[60]

Since the 1870s, the cattle drives from Texas to the railroad shipping points in Kansas had become larger and larger. Initially conducted over the Texas Road through the Choctaw and Creek Nations, the eastern part of the Indian Territory, new trails in the west had been opened and herds of two to three thousand were being moved, grazing as they went. The pressures for change were mounting. The white settlers in the Five Civilized Nations were almost doubling every year, reaching 25,000 by 1884.[61] Indians were demanding territorial government instead of reliance upon the courts of neighboring states. The large numbers of whites intermarrying with Indians, the adoption of white customs, and the growing wealth of Indians and mixed-bloods who were renting tribal lands to whites changed the character of the Five Civilized Nations. These factors, combined with the lobbying efforts of the cattlemen and railroad interests, were moving toward the reduced sovereignty of the Nations and the eventual elimination of them altogether. Therefore, it is not surprising that the GC&SF right-of-way bill would introduce major changes to the status quo.[62] Senator Coke later described it as "the most liberal bill of the kind that he ever knew of." The main provisions were summarized as follows:

> It imposes no conditions upon the company, except that the proposed extension shall enter the territory at some point in Cooke County. After entering the territory the company can build in any direction it chooses and make any connections which will be the most desirable. Three years of time is granted, in which only 100 miles of road in the territory must be built, which secures the right of way for all time to

come. The road will be laid off in sections of 25 miles each, with the nominal approval of the Secretary of the Interior, and may extend in any direction.[63]

The chiefs doubtlessly would have agreed with Senator Coke's estimation of bill. They spelled out their objections deliberately in a five-part letter to Congress. First, they challenged the amount of land taken, the amount of compensation, and the fact that the Cherokee treaty did not permit such confiscations whereas the Choctaw Treaty did. Second, they challenged the provision granting the right to settle on the right-of-way, claiming that this would ultimately lead to the breakup of the five Indian nations. Third, they protested damage suits being settled in adjacent states rather than in the Indian Territory as with the existing road, the MKT. Fourth, the power of taxation was retained by Congress, whereas in the neighboring states of Kansas and Texas, such power was held by the state. Finally, the chiefs referred to the decision of the Supreme Court (18 Howard, page 100) that the measure of power of the [Cherokee nation] government is only limited by the express terms of treaty limitation.[64]

In conclusion, the chiefs stated: "In the territories Congress merely grants a right of way through public lands; but here they claim the right, if this bill is passed, to make another disposition of property they conveyed to us and placed under our jurisdiction. This proposed law further overrides our laws regulating the mode of obtaining ties and other material. These measures are full of wrongs to us, and of danger both to us and the country, and we beg of you to carefully consider them, and not to permit a violation of the treaty pledges made to us by the United States."[65]

The House of Representatives passed the bill on May 30, 1884, making it the fourth right-of-way granted. On June 19, the Senate voted 34−11 in favor of Senator Coke's motion to consider the bill, thus giving it preference over all others except appropriations. On June 21 the Senate passed the bill without injurious amendments and sent it back to the House for concurrence. Senator Coke was cited for his able management, assisted by Senators Maxey and Plumb. The *Daily News* also reported that "Mr. Walter Gresham's friends are congratulating him on his success."[66]

PRESIDENT ARTHUR SIGNS THE BILL

On July 1, the *Daily News* announced that the bill had been passed and had gone to President Chester Arthur for signature. The Washington correspondent of the *Daily News* proclaimed: "Major [*sic*] Gresham is pronounced by the Texas delegation a perfect success in managing business before Congress." The Washington correspondent was equally enthusiastic about Gresham in reporting the signing of the bill by President Arthur on July 4. He said:

> The success in securing the enactment of this measure at this session, when so many bills affecting railroad interests have either failed or gone over to the next session, is due, in a great messier [*sic*], to the zeal and ability of Mr. Walter Gresham. In its management he was active and untiring in his efforts, and by the exercise of his usual good judgment succeeded in winning the confidence of members and enlisting a strong support for his bill. He was aided earnestly and efficiently throughout by Messrs. Wellborn, Throckmorton, Ochiltree and the balance of the Texas congressmen.[67]

Heretofore, Gresham, as attorney for the railroad, had been involved principally in obtaining right-of-way, and, at least in comparison with the Sealy brothers, was an obscure personality in the management of the GC&SF. But, as a by-product of the passage of this important legislation, Gresham emerged from the shadows. His experience before Congress was to serve Galveston well in the near future in pursuit of the deep water channel, and on into the future as a state legislator, congressman, and chairman of the Deep Water Committee for a number of years. In fact, his newfound status was evident the next day when he, now "promoted" to colonel, was the subject of an interview upon his return from Washington. Gresham was neither reluctant nor coy about stating his views regarding the future of the GC&SF to the reporter. "I would recommend building through the Territory to the Kansas line where we would find no difficulty in making favorable arrangements for eastern freights, and could extend northward through the grain regions of Kansas and Nebraska," said Gresham.[68]

"When Galveston succeeds in getting thirty feet of water—which I am confident we will obtain under the Eads plan, and which plan I am confident Congress will adopt at the next term—the route to the sea over the line above indicated would give to Galveston an advantage of about 16 cents a bushel on wheat exported from those great grain-growing sections," he explained. Gresham continued: "The great breeding grounds of Southwest Texas will find by this extension of the Santa Fe its best and most direct line for sending its stock to the territory composed of New Mexico, Colorado, and Wyoming. The Santa Fe will shorten the present drive very materially."[69]

It had been reported that the board of directors was planning the issuance of first and second mortgage bonds to finance the extension. How-

ever, at a special stockholders meeting called on June 11, 1884, the stockholders failed to approve the proposition of the board. When asked about
the recent action of the stockholders in voting down the issuance of mortgage bonds, Gresham was positive in his response. "The proposition submitted by the directory to the stockholders for the construction of 200
miles of road did not contemplate this line," he pointed out. He added
that he did not believe that the negative vote would deter the directors
from submitting another proposition because of the value of the franchise.
Construction costs were very low now, he explained, and savings on coal
obtained in the territory could pay for the fixed charges on 100 miles of
the extension.[70]

Gresham's prediction regarding the board's attitude toward the extension northward came true when the board passed the following resolution
at its regular meeting on September 8, 1884: "That the General Manager
be instructed to send an Engineer to examine the country on the proposed
line of road from Ft. Worth through the Indian Territory to the State of
Kansas, with directions to report on the most feasible route, the nature
and topography of the country, prospects, if any, for a supply of coal in the
line, and on all matters relating to the cost of the road, and capabilities of
the country through which it will run."[71]

While the granting of the right-of-way through the Indian Territory
may have been the final blow to the Gould forces, to some extent the
agreement may be attributed to the declining business conditions in 1884.
A late cotton crop began to affect the earnings of the southwestern railroads in August. A short crop in 1884 would be the third bad season in a
row for the cotton industry. In addition, a decline in cattle prices from the
1879 peak was severely hurting the state's second largest industry.

In the annual report to the stockholders, on October 7, 1884, President
George Sealy described conditions this way: "The year's business in Texas
has been disastrous to all railroad companies. The very short crops, together with the great depression in all kinds of trade, have reduced our
gross earning, so that in your next general statement there will be very
little surplus left the stockholders. The small business in Texas the past
year induced unhealthy competition which resulted in lowering the rates
for carrying freights when full rates should have been received."[72]

JOHN SEALY'S DEATH

The year 1884 had been disastrous for President George Sealy in a more
personal way. His brother John died August 29 at the age of sixty-one,

and his partner in the Ball, Hutchings & Company, George Ball, died March 13 at the age of sixty-three. Apparently George Sealy, after five years of intensive involvement with the GC&SF, tried to withdraw to devote more time to the banking and other interests. In January of that year, Webster Snyder, then general manager of the Louisville, Evansville & St. Louis Railroad, was brought in as general manager of the GC&SF. At that time, George Sealy stated that the plan was for John Sealy to move up to replace him as president so that he could resign. Instead, it was John Sealy who resigned to rest, apparently suffering from bad health. After both deaths, Sealy found his situation even worse without the presence of the two senior partners. Consequently, in his report to the stockholders of October 7, he tendered his resignation, stating, "I will not be a candidate for re-election, nor can I serve if elected." Nevertheless, at the next meeting of the board of directors, the board unanimously reelected him president of the company, "a merited compliment to Mr. Sealy's pronounced executive and administrative ability," as the *News* described it.[73]

By November, the impact of the hard times described by Sealy to the stockholders began to be felt. Personnel cuts were made throughout the organization, including the clerical staff in the general offices. In addition, salaries of those retained were reduced 10 to 30 percent. In some departments, the reductions totaled 40 to 50 percent of annual expenses.[74]

As if these circumstances were not enough, the commissioner of Indian Affairs and the Cherokee Nation were opposing the right-of-ways granted by Congress. According to the commissioner, "The Cherokee Nation insists that its property can not be taken and given to a private corporation of any State by Congress, and that the courts of the country will not sustain such a seizure or violation of the contract made by the United States in its treaties with the Cherokee Nation." The *Daily News* article, quoting the *St. Louis Republican,* concluded: "It is probable that the consent of the Indians might be obtained for a fair consideration, but they are likely to resist the attempt of Congress to assert the right of eminent domain in their territory, and should the Supreme Court sustain them, as seems probable in view of recent decisions treating the tribes as independent nations, it may be several years before this important and desirable connection can be arranged for by treaty."[75]

Thus, despite the fact that the GC&SF may have had the upper hand in the war with the Gould system at the end of 1884, other external factors were making things very difficult for the company, its directory, and its president. Since the right-of-way of the GC&SF actually proceeded through the Chickasaw Nation, the Oklahoma Lands, and the Cherokee Outlet, which the Cherokees had given up in 1866, perhaps the Cherokees

decided not to fight the legislation passed in 1884 for both the GC&SF and
the Southern Kansas, waiting for a better opportunity. This was provided
when Congress approved the Kansas & Arkansas Valley Railway on June 1,
1886, to run from Fort Smith up the Arkansas Valley, which was the Cherokee border, to Kansas. The Cherokees objected to the road and carried
the case to the Supreme Court, only to lose. The Congress's establishment
of the right of eminent domain in the GC&SF act, in effect, opened the
door to any railroad wishing to cross the Indian Territory and the Five
Nations. Now only the unfavorable business climate stood in the way of
the GC&SF's march north.

CHAPTER SIX

GOULD STYMIED
First the Pool, Then the Sale

In his report to the board of directors of March 3, 1885, President Sealy described the financial condition for the past year as unsatisfactory owing to a combination of "crop failure, a panic, and a very great and general depression in trade, such as we have not had in Texas during the past twenty years." He admitted the financial condition was worsened by large expenditures for roadbed and motive power that were made in anticipation of at least average business, and pointed out that monthly operating expenses had been reduced by $30,000 per month to help correct the balance sheet.[1]

Moreover, he added, the situation was further worsened by the failure of the parties to the previous year's rate agreement to maintain the rates for a full month following the agreement. The crop shortage resulted in rate reductions to keep business, even if carried at no profit. "The result was that there has been no regular rates upon any road in Texas during the past season," Sealy reported. To remedy the problem, Sealy suggested that "an effort should be made by the incoming Board to so manage that an agreement shall be entered into between the General Managers of the different roads in Texas, to establish fair rates to all points and deprive Freight Agents of authority to deviate from them without the consent of all parties to the agreement under penalty of dismissal from office or position."[2]

On April 6, 1885, it was announced that representatives of the two rail/sea networks operating in the Gulf of Mexico—the Southern Pacific and Morgan lines on one hand and the GC&SF and Mallory lines on the other—had met in New Orleans and agreed upon rates that would enable all four companies to avoid operating at small profit margins.[3]

Negotiations expanding the parties to include the Southern Pacific apparently started soon after the New Orleans meeting. General manager Alexander C. Hutchinson reported to Collis P. Huntington in New York that the major problem encountered was that, as a committee was collecting statements of tonnage and revenues upon which to base percentages, the Texas & St. Louis refused to provide any data, which was tantamount to withdrawing. Hutchinson stated that it would be impractical to leave the Texas & St. Louis free to lower rates. "It seems strange to me that Mr. Sealy does not appreciate this state of things," he said. He stated that Hoxie, representing the Missouri Pacific, had called a meeting in Galveston, which now would have to concern itself with maintaining rates rather than a pool arrangement, because of the action of the Texas & St. Louis.[4]

Apparently Sealy was holding back even on a rate agreement, because on July 2, 1885, Huntington wrote to him requesting that the GC&SF restore rates regardless of what the Texas & St. Louis did.[5] At a board meeting early on July 13, 1885, Sealy gave the directors a brief outline of the basis for a pooling agreement reached at a meeting of the presidents of the four Texas roads in New York on June 26, 1885. The agreement would cover a period of five or ten years during which the said roads were to work offensively and defensively together. If the percentages in the pool were not otherwise agreed upon, they would be arbitrated, and a pool commissioner would be selected to make rates and monthly settlements. The motion in favor of the pooling arrangement was unanimously approved.[6]

On July 3, the *Railway Gazette* announced, perhaps prematurely, that a pooling agreement had been reached between the Missouri Pacific, the Southern Pacific, the GC&SF, and the Houston & Texas Central, not mentioning the Texas & St. Louis but stating only that "it is expected that the minor roads in Texas will also unite with the pool." The next day the *New York Financial Chronicle* reported that the agreement was semi-officially announced and outlined the basic principles of what would later be known as the Texas Traffic Association.[7]

Illustrative of the problem the railroads were facing, Hutchinson wrote to Huntington on July 4, was the fact that the Texas & Pacific, part of the Missouri Pacific system, had cut rates while the presidents were approaching the agreement. Hutchinson stated his belief that retaliation should not be immediate so that top management would have a chance to stop the violation of agreements by subordinates. Otherwise, all of the rate structures would fall apart.[8] In his reply, Huntington offered the opinion that Hoxie probably made himself unavailable when such occasions arose, and added that when he attempted to see Gould in New York, his office would reply that he was out of town or that they did not know where he was.[9]

A commissioner with absolute authority over freight departments of each road would be the only solution to the problem of evasive answers being offered by Hoxie, Hayes, and W. H. Newman, suggested Hutchinson in his next letter to Huntington.[10]

On July 15, representatives of the Texas roads, including the Texas & St. Louis, met in Galveston to begin the process of ironing out the details of the association, to be known as the Texas Pool. Those present included the following:

Southern Pacific: Alexander C. Hutchinson, general manager; J. G. Schriever, traffic manager; C. C. Gibbs, general freight agent; and C. L. Queyrouze, assistant auditor.

Houston & Texas Central: C. L. Dillingham, receiver; J. Waldo, agent for the receiver; Dan Ripley, general freight agent; and A. Faulkner, general passenger agent.

Texas & St. Louis: L. B. Fish, treasurer; and A. S. Dodge, general freight agent.

Missouri Pacific: H. M. Hoxie, vice president, and W. H. Newman, master of transportation.

Gulf, Colorado & Santa Fe: George Sealy, president; Webster Snyder, general manager; and Oscar G. Murray, general freight agent.[11]

Sealy was elected president of the conference, and committees were named to examine and report on the various subjects that would come before the conference. Three days later the *Daily News* reported that little progress had been made, in spite of day and night sessions, because of the diversity of interests to be reconciled.[12]

DIFFICULT ISSUES ARISE

The first issue to arise pertained to the inclusion of business that originated outside the state. Huntington notified Hutchinson that Sealy had requested attorney Percy Pyne in New York to ask Huntington and Gould for their interpretation of the agreement on this issue. Admitting that he knew little about the details of railroad rates and traffic patterns, Huntington told Hutchinson that the matter was up to him, although he failed to see any reason that business originating outside of Texas and passing through should go into the pool.[13]

At this point Huntington informed Hutchinson that merchant Robert Hawley had positive proof that the Missouri Pacific was cutting rates, even while negotiations were taking place, and Huntington expressed his exasperation at what it would take "to hold Hoxie down to fair and square dealings." Nevertheless, following Hutchinson's earlier advice, he told Hawley not to to cut any rates until he had orders to do so.[14]

On July 20, Hutchinson wrote a lengthy letter to Huntington review-ing the progress, or lack thereof, of the negotiations and defining the is-sues, most of which involved the positions taken by Sealy. After initially informing the group that the understanding reached by the presidents in New York on July 3 included all business handled by the roads, Sealy backed off and agreed that only traffic originating or terminating within the state, as well as intrastate traffic, would be included in the pool.[15]

Determining the base year for the adjustment of earnings also presented difficulty, since both the Southern Pacific and GC&SF objected to 1884, which was a bad year for them, while the Missouri Pacific preferred 1884. Hutchinson reported that after much discussion, 1883 was finally selected to serve as the basis for determining earnings.

Whereas Sealy seemed to have achieved most of his objectives on the first two issues, he lost on the third, and most serious, according to Hutchinson. Sealy proposed that any new road under construction should be included in the earnings at one-half the earnings of completed road. In view of the fact that the new road would not be completed until the end of 1885, Hutchinson took the position that it was simply impos-sible to decide upon the earnings of a new road, and that the matter would have to be left to arbitration at the end of 1886. Since Hoxie agreed with Hutchinson on this matter and such issues required unanimous consent, the conference was faced with the possibility of breaking up until Sealy finally relented and accepted arbitration as a means of dealing with the new road.

No sooner had one disruptive issue been settled than another arose, this time with Hoxie being the culprit. When it came time to define the executive committee, who along with the commissioner would handle the business of the pool, Hoxie maintained that the Missouri Pacific and the Texas & Pacific were separate concerns and each entitled to a repre-sentative on the committee, leading Hutchinson to propose the same for the Houston & Texas Central and the Texas Central, both owned by the Southern Pacific. Sealy objected that the combination of those four com-panies could dominate the seven-man committee. According to Hutch-inson, "Hoxie stood out against this and also refused to accede to his hav-ing but one representative in the Committee," and for some time it seemed as though the meeting would break up. In fact Hoxie moved to adjourn sine die, but Sealy finally proposed to allow the four lines to have the four votes, as Hoxie proposed, but that in all questions the majority should be five instead of four. Hoxie finally agreed to this solution, but Hutchinson warned Huntington that the conference might yet come to a halt over the issue of who the commissioner would be.[16]

George Sealy was again the holdout. J. Waldo of the H&TC was nominated by Hoxie and received all of the votes on the first ballot except that of the GC&SF. Hutchinson did not dwell upon the details of the objection by Sealy but informed Huntington that "finally after many ballots and long talk and discussion (over two days) between Mr. Sealy on one side and Mr. Hoxie and myself on the other, the former accepted him." Hutchinson felt that it was absolutely necessary to have someone with long experience in the state who would be familiar with the peculiarities of traffic in Texas.[17]

Again, perhaps Hutchinson's worst fears were overstated, for on July 24 the *Daily News* announced the formation of the Texas Traffic Association and the selection of J. Waldo as commissioner with offices located in Galveston.[18] However, there were privately expressed concerns regarding the ratification by the GC&SF Board of Directors. In a letter to Huntington, Hutchinson observed that "Mr. Sealy will have great difficulty in controlling his own Directors. He himself, has broader views, understands the situation and appreciates the necessity of his road accepting the position belonging to it, in connection with the other lines in the State. The Directors were large bondholders and some of them sold their bonds and invested in the stock, hence they are very much discouraged and are inclined to look upon the gloomy side."[19]

Hoxie also had some doubts. In a letter to A. L. Hopkins, the Missouri Pacific first vice president, he stated: "If the Gulf, Colorado and Santa Fe people approve of the new agreement, by their Board of Directors, which I hope they will—although there appears to be some doubt of it—it will prove a very remunerative contract for the rail lines in Texas. The Santa Fe people did not take in the whole scope of their agreement, or think out the question sufficiently, to see the effect it would have on their local business."[20]

Speculation regarding what the GC&SF would do turned to rumor, and Huntington soon found it necessary to question Hutchinson as to whether or not they had pulled out of the agreement.[21] The rumor was not without substance; the *Daily News* reported the next day that the GC&SF Board of Directors was proposing the right to withdraw from the agreement after one year, with sixty days' notice, instead of being firmly committed for the full five years of the agreement.[22] It was true that the board, meeting August 3, 1885, had passed a resolution to that effect introduced by John H. Hutchings that passed by a 5–3 vote.[23] The executive committee had rejected the proposal, but Sealy offered that the matter should be taken up by the presidents and announced plans to leave for New York for that purpose.[24]

On August 5, the sole member of the conference remaining in Galveston, the Texas & St. Louis line's Fish, was interviewed by the *Daily News*. In his opinion, the disagreement was owing to the belief that the "directory of the Gulf, Colorado and Santa Fe did not thoroughly understand the details of the pool, in which he could see nothing detrimental to their interest." When asked if concessions had been made to the GC&SF, Fish replied: "Concessions as to rate were made to the Gulf, Colorado and Santa Fe, and concessions which, in my opinion, were exceedingly advantageous to the interests of that road and to Galveston. This was in reference to rates upon cotton, and the concession that was made to the Gulf, Colorado and Santa Fe in this particular would, I think, have brought two-thirds or four-fifths of the entire cotton crop of this season over the Gulf, Colorado and Santa Fe and through Galveston." [25]

Upon his return to New Orleans, Hutchinson reported to Huntington that "Mr. Sealy's position in this whole matter has been unfortunate, as it is clear his Directors have gone back on him, apparently without any valid reason; as it has always been admitted there was no legal method by which any of the parties could be prevented from withdrawing when they saw fit to do so." Hutchinson went on to explain that it had been Hoxie who, in the name of harmony, had proposed the cotton rate concession for the GC&SF, and, apparently very put out with the action of the Santa Fe Board, suggested to Huntington that the other parties might proceed with the pool without the GC&SF and act offensively and defensively against them. "It is very difficult to account for the action of the Santa Fe people, unless perhaps, it is because Mr. Sealy is so unfortunate as to have a Board of Directors composed of merchants who are in no wise familiar with the operation of railroad traffic," he observed. [26]

Since the cotton and wholesale merchants who largely comprised the GC&SF board were among the most successful in Texas and had to be involved with railroad rates as one of their principal costs of doing business, one cannot help but speculate as to whether the board differences with President Sealy, who after all was not permitted to resign the year before, were a negotiating ploy intended to squeeze the most out of the pool agreement. The evidence of real disagreement between the board and Sealy is lacking. In fact, Hutchinson offered a similar interpretation in his next letter to Huntington the following day. He explained to Huntington, "It seems the Santa Fe people were very much surprised at the unexpected reception by our committee, of their resolution. It was introduced into their Board by Mr. Hutchins [*sic*], of Ball, Hutchins [*sic*] & Co, and it was supposed the effect would be to delay matters and perhaps induce concessions on the part of the other Companies. They had no idea it would result in refusal on the part of the latter, and consequently break up the meeting."[27]

NEGOTIATING TACTICS

Sealy, apparently going along with the tactic of his business partner, Hutchings, even stopped attending the meetings of the conference, sending instead his general manager, Webster Snyder, who was instructed to look wise and remain silent. This tactic only served to further aggravate Hutchinson, who told Sealy, "I will not attend any meeting in the future on this subject, until thoroughly satisfied that the parties representing the Santa Fe, were authorized to act, and that their action would be sustained by their Directory." As to a meeting of the presidents, Hutchinson recommended in ever stronger terms that the agreement was complete and that all that remained was for ratification by the GC&SF.[28]

Gould, Huntington, and Sealy met in New York on August 12 to resolve the issue. The next day, the *New York Times* carried a dispatch from Galveston stating that Sealy had telegraphed his board that all had agreed to the proposed withdrawal after a year with sixty days' notice.[29] This time the *Daily News* seems to have gotten its facts wrong; the Sealy telegram read in the board meeting on the twelfth said:

> Parties decline the one year provision on the grounds that we cannot more than get into operation under it before it may be ended. They consent to arbitrate any question that may arise by any part to the contract that cannot be adjusted satisfactorily through the Executive Committee.
>
> I advise approving contract with arbitration clause, or perhaps I can get them to make and maintain rates outside of any pool.[30]

The board then approved a resolution by a 5–2 vote to accept the pool agreement with the arbitration clause included. The next day both the *Times* and the *Daily News* reported that the five-year term remained, without the sixty-day clause, but that the agreement now contained a provision that all disagreements between the parties would be submitted to arbitration. Explained the *Times:* "This prevents it [the GC&SF] from being crowded to the wall by the majority interests in the pool and admits of the preservation of its independence."[31] In other words, the sixty-day withdrawal clause may have been used as a negotiating card to obtain the arbitration of differences.

On August 14, notification went out to each of the general managers, stating: "Differences in the Texas Traffic Association having been adjusted, the Commissioner and the Executive Committee can perfect the organization. Signed: C. P. Huntington, Charles Dillingham, Jay Gould and George Sealy."[32]

Thus President Sealy found himself now an equal to those who had spent the last five years in various efforts either to squeeze him out or to buy him out. If Sealy's only goal was a return to profitability, it had been achieved. If there were other goals still in the back of his mind, and prior events suggested that there may have been, they would have to be revealed at a later date.

Huntington, in the process of completing the pool agreement, displayed a bit of "above the battle" whimsy to the whole affair. On August 13, the same article that appeared in the *New York Times* was published in a New Orleans paper, causing Hutchinson immediately to fire off a telegram to Huntington complaining about the Santa Fe people giving information to the press: "Sealy should put a stop to such miserable indiscretion, which is more like action of children than men," he stated. The telegram was followed that same day by a letter (which included the clipped newspaper article) describing how secrets of negotiations always appeared in the paper the next morning during the negotiations in Galveston.[33]

In his reply on the seventeenth, Huntington agreed that it was a great shame that the Santa Fe people talked to the press before a contract was completed. "But," he continued, "as I understand it, the G.C.& S.F. Ry. Co. is controlled by town meetings and I never heard of such a meeting where the proceedings were withheld from the public. Probably there never will be. It is, I suppose, difficult now as of old to build a city upon a hill and hide it."[34]

The executive committee met in Galveston on August 24, 1885, to initiate the operations of the pool. Its first action was to fix rates on cotton from Dallas at $3.25 per bale to Houston, $3.50 per bale to Galveston, and $3.75 to St. Louis or New Orleans.[35] On the same day, a called meeting of the GC&SF Board was held to take action on a request from J. Waldo to have the location of the offices of the Texas Traffic Association moved from Galveston to Houston. The board discussed the request, voted unanimously against it, and adjourned. Another called meeting was held on September 5, and again the request was rejected.[36]

On September 5 the freight agents met with the executive committee to complete the determination of rates, adding those for grain, lumber, livestock, wool, hides, and general merchandise to those already established for cotton. The executive committee also decided that the commissioner's offices would be located in Houston, thus changing the provision of the signed agreement.[37]

Again, Hutchinson's report to Huntington was more informative than the *Daily News* coverage. As it was, something of a crisis was created by the Santa Fe action because Commissioner Waldo resigned. Snyder, again sitting in for Sealy, did not vote for the resolution authorizing the location at Houston. During the midday adjournment of the meeting, Dillingham and Hutchinson went to see Sealy to discuss the matter. Sealy could only offer that, while he had no objections, his board had passed a resolution against it. Dillingham and Hutchinson argued that since a two-thirds vote of the executive committee could discharge the commissioners, a two-thirds vote could also change the location of the offices.[38] Apparently no further resistance was offered, and during the afternon session, Waldo withdrew his resignation and the committee proceeded to draw up his contract, which Sealy signed the next day.

Hutchinson, however, did not pass up the opportunity to further express his dim view of the Santa Fe people and the situation in Galveston. He wrote: "It would simply have been impractical to have kept the office at Galveston. Gossip in the place is something fearful and everything that is done at meetings is known on the streets in an hour. Sealy's Board has a way of getting together every two hours and passing upon the acts of the President, and apparently nothing is done except upon their actions. You can't imagine what a nuisance and annoyance this must be."[39]

To later critics of corporate management who bemoaned the loss of control by boards of directors and stockholders to the corporate executives, the situation condemned by Hutchinson might appear as the golden age of American business when the modern corporation operated as it was designed to, with boards of directors representing stockholders and actually maintaining control of the company instead of abdicating power to "hired hands."

With what was probably thought to be the final internal squabble now settled, the association began to operate and issued its Circular No. 1 on September 15, implementing a resolution passed by the executive committee at the September 4 meeting in Galveston prohibiting the payment of commissions to agent of connecting lines. This practice, condemned by all but the ticket agents receiving the commissions, was a subject of widespread controversy. The executive committee showed its seriousness on the matter by announcing that the sale of the tickets by an offending line would be discontinued.[40]

By mid-October the commissioner's office was established and operating from quarters in W. H. Coyle's new building on Franklin Street in Houston. An impressed Houston correspondent of the *Daily News* reported that he was "astonished at the beauty and usefulness of the establishment. Commissioner Waldo's office is in the south corner. It is furnished with Brussels carpet, is supplied with modern business appliances and is airy, well-lighted and comfortable." [41]

The October meeting of the association was held in St. Louis, and even Hutchinson at this point felt that it "will work harmoniously, as all parties seem bent on having it so." [42] Cooperation was even breaking out at the higher levels. Hoxie reported an exchange of correspondence between Gould and Huntington, expressing their determination to make every effort to carry out the commissioner's order abolishing commissions. [43] Except for the main issue itself—whether or not the Texas roads would cooperate or continue ruinous competition—the negotiations of the association were generally not reported to the public and pertained to the intricacies of rates interesting mainly to railroadmen. [44]

NEW OBSTACLES ARISE

Operations of both the new Traffic Association and the GC&SF Railroad were temporarily threatened when labor unrest in the industry spread to Galveston and the Knights of Labor struck after demands were not met. The strike turned ugly and almost resulted in a violent conflict between the armed strikers and a *posse comitatus* of directors and militia units. Last-minute negotiations between leaders of both sides finally ended the crisis. The press coverage made no connections between the strike and the Texas Traffic Association agreement that had just been concluded. However, had a prolonged strike been permitted to paralyze the GC&SF, there would have been little need for Huntington and Gould to have made any concessions to stabilize the rate situation in Texas. The strike may have been timed to take place just as the GC&SF was on the verge of a major victory, and not in any position to let a strike deprive it of the rewards. Faced with increasing revenues under the terms of the pool, the GC&SF directors could well afford to grant the concessions in return for the assured rates and percentage of the traffic.

The *Daily News* was very fair in its treatment of the strike and the strikers, although the opposite may have been expected, since publisher Alfred H. Belo certainly counted himself with the GC&SF directors. Neither side was disparaged in the coverage of the strike events; in fact, it sounded sometimes as if the reporter reacted joyfully in relating the triumphs of the strikers in killing the steam engines right under the noses of the armed posse and militia. The attitude of the paper toward organized labor in general was expressed in an editorial that ran at the height of the strike that maintained that the protective tariff sought by manufacturers was the root of the labor troubles since it encouraged unions to strike for a tariff on foreign labor. Arguing that government had nothing of its own to give and that benefits accorded one group had to be at the expense of another, the *Daily News* reasoned that the workingmen could not be faulted for seeking the same protection from foreign competition that the manufacturers were seeking.[45]

Before 1885 was over, Sealy had resumed the drawn-out discussions with the AT&SF, where the very aggressive William B. Strong was now president. In reply to a Strong letter, Sealy replied on December 4, "I wrote to you yesterday to the effect that our people would be willing to consolidate on a fair basis, and for you to name a time and place to meet to discuss the question."[46] Sealy went on to point out that in writing the letter he had forgotten that a meeting at the end of the month would interfere with both Christmas and the expected arrival of a new child, and suggested meeting by December 15 or waiting until January. (As it turned out, Rebecca Willis Sealy was born December 17, 1885.)[47]

On February 9, 1886, Strong wrote to Sealy offering a counterproposal to a GC&SF offer made since Sealy's December letter. The GC&SF proposed an equal exchange of stock between the two companies. In addition, the GC&SF wanted to build another 300 miles of road to carry out the agreement no sooner than twelve months. In his counterproposal, Strong agreed to the 300 miles (200 miles north from Fort Worth and 100 miles from Dallas to Paris) and reiterated his previous position: "and with this concession I now renew my proposition that on the basis of $12,000 per mile of first mortgage bonds, $5,000 per mile of second mortgage bonds and $8,000 per mile of capital stock we will exchange the capital stock at the rate of three shares of Atchison stock for four shares of your Company's."[48]

As might be expected in a letter that is part of a negotiating process, Strong argued the difficulty of convincing his stockholders to approve a deal on any other terms when the Atchison, unlike the GC&SF, had been earning 6 percent on its capital stock for many years and was bonded at a very low rate per mile. Because of the strong potential for the AT&SF stock to appreciate over the next twelve months, he doubted the possibility of obtaining the directors' concurrence to delay the agreement very long. He also pointed out the profits to be made by the GC&SF from the construction of the additional 300 miles and the acquisition of that much more stock as further reasons that the Atchison stockholders would not agree to a one-for-one trade.[49]

There is no known documentation of the further progress of the negotiations until the agreement signed by Strong and Sealy on March 3, 1886,
providing the terms of sale, or stock swap. The AT&SF agreed to "assume
all of said bonded indebtedness, including interest thereon, and to exchange an even amount of their stock for that of the Gulf, Colorado and
Santa Fe Railway Company stock up to the extent of eight thousand dollars per mile, not to exceed one thousand miles in all, or say, in all, eight
million of stock, as hereinafter stated."[50]

The contract went on to state that the GC&SF would present
$4,560,000 for exchange as early as possible, and that another $1,140,000,
for a total of $5,700,000, would be presented for exchange between May 15
and July 1, 1886. It also provided that an additional $2,300,000 of stock
would be given by the AT&SF to the GC&SF, making a total of $8,000,000
in all by January 1, 1887.[51] On March 15 the following GC&SF directors
signed a ratification of the agreement: George Sealy, Richard S. Willis,
Waters S. Davis, John C. Wallis, John H. Hutchings, Harris Kempner,
Leon H. Blum, Walter Gresham, John D. Rogers, William L. Moody,
and Henry Rosenberg.[52]

On March 30, 1886, an additional document was signed by Presidents
Sealy and Strong "in explanation and amendment of, and to carry into effect, the Agreement made March 3, 1886." This document obligated Sealy
to deliver by April 20 at least $3,500,000 of the total $4,560,000 of GC&SF
stock, at which time the AT&SF would exchange its stock share for share.
In addition, the document contained this clause, which would later become a source of bitter division: "It is agreed; that when the railroad shall
have been completed to Purcell, making in all about seven hundred miles,
that all liabilities above those for usual current expenses, shall be covered
by an issue of first mortgage bonds not exceeding $12,000 and of second
mortgage bonds not exceeding $5000 per mile of constructed main line of
road except liabilities incurred for labor or for property purchased and materials on hand for the construction of road additional to the 700 miles of
road mentioned above."[53]

MORGAN JONES ACCEPTS CHALLENGE

The agreement to build the additional 300 miles resulted in one of the
most interesting episodes in the GC&SF history. President Sealy and chief
engineer Walter Justin Sherman were faced with building 300 miles of
road in a year, a very difficult task. They turned to Morgan Jones, one
of the fabulous figures of Texas railroad history, to get the job done. Jones,

with his partner, Hugh Burns, had already contracted for building the Fort Worth-Red River extension.[54] Jones was reluctant to take on the additional task, but Sealy and Sherman offered him a $100,000 bonus if he completed the job on time, and he finally agreed to take it on.[55]

Jones placed one of his previous associates, Dan Carey, in charge of grading, made Al Haynes responsible for bridge building, and put General M. F. Thomas, a former Union brigade commander, over track laying. As the pressures of meeting the deadline grew, Thomas became discouraged and quit. Jones took over for him and persisted with the job, beating the deadline by two and one-half days, as the GC&SF's first locomotive pulled into Purcell on April 26, 1887. On June 18, 1887, through trains began to operate between Kansas City and Galveston.[56]

The deal did not have a happy ending, however. The GC&SF maintained that some of the rock and masonry work was unsatisfactory and refused to let Jones complete the job. Convinced that the GC&SF was seeking a way to back out of the promised bonus, Jones turned to a board of arbitration.

The board held hearings for three weeks in Dallas and awarded Jones $60,000 for completing on schedule. Angered by the proceedings, Jones refused to complete the masonry work, and the board recommended withholding the remaining $40,000. The quarrelling was so unpleasant to Jones that he never again undertook building someone else's railroad.[57]

The driving of the last spike connecting the Gulf, Colorado & Santa Fe with its parent company, the Atchison, Topeka & Santa Fe, at Purcell in the Indian Territory (Oklahoma), located on the Canadian River 100 miles north of the Texas border, opened the way for ending the management transition period for the two companies. Following the sale in March, 1886, Sealy was named a director of the AT&SF, one of four non-Bostonians among the thirteen directors.[58] The board chose to have GC&SF officers Sealy, president; Richard Willis, vice president; and Waters Davis, treasurer, continue to serve through the transition period until completion of the extension. This was in accordance with the policy expressed in the annual report of the Atchison, Topeka & Santa Fe for the year ending December 31, 1886.[59] Sealy, Willis, and Davis resigned their positions on May 14, 1887, at a board of directors meeting in Galveston, completing the transition to total control and active management of the GC&SF by the AT&SF. Strong replaced Sealy as president, C. W. Smith replaced Willis, and Thomas W. Jackson replaced Davis. Sealy continued, however, as a director of the AT&SF.[60]

The AT&SF officers and directors from Boston, including former president A. W. Nickerson and founder C. K. Holliday of Kansas, arrived in Texas on May 13 to look over their new property. Arriving at Dallas, they traveled the extensions to Cleburne and Honey Grove. The next day they started for Galveston, with time taken out for a trip over the extension to Ballinger in West Texas. Festivities planned during their visit to Galveston had to be canceled after it was announced they could stay only long enough to hold the directors' meeting that accomplished the election of the new GC&SF officers. Sealy's resignation at the meeting was accompanied by the following resolution, introduced by Strong and seconded by Nickerson:

> Whereas Mr. George Sealy is about to retire from presidency of this company; and
> Whereas it is the desire of the board to record their high appreciation of the fidelity and ability with which Mr. Sealy has managed their affairs of the company during the whole time of his official connection with it; and
> Whereas we regard it as largely due to his untiring efforts in behalf of this company that its line has increased from about 60 miles to 1000 miles at the present time, and has been transformed from an unimportant local road to a great thoroughfare, and a part of a system connecting Galveston with the Missouri and Mississippi Valley, and the great lakes; be it therefore
> Resolved, that the thanks of this board are tendered Mr. Sealy for his great and successful service to this company, and that we here express our best for this future prosperity and good fortune.[61]

The *Daily News* acknowledged that "there may be some regret felt at the retirement of the local directory and managerial interest, but this regret cannot be long lived in presence of the fact that the management which has assumed control is among the most broad gauged and liberal known to the American railway system." The position of Galveston now as an AT&SF terminal, the increased pressure for deep water, and the potential for new steamship connections added up to "a great deal" for the city, a change to be welcomed by all.[62]

BENEFITS TO GALVESTON

Those looking for benefits to emerge from the AT&SF acquisition had only to wait for the Bostonians to return home. On May 23, 1887, it was announced that the GC&SF would build from Dallas to Gainesville if Dallas would acquire the right-of-way. The businessmen of Dallas met the same day to organize committees to begin the solicitation of the landowners along the route. From Paris it was announced that the GC&SF extension to that city from Ladonia had been completed. And from New York it was reported that the AT&SF was negotiating for the St. Louis & Chicago to obtain that direct connection.[63] On June 12 the *Daily News* announced that the first through passenger train over the Galveston-Kansas City route would leave the city at 4 P.M. The train, described as the finest ever to service Galveston, would be composed of all new equipment and handsomely decorated in honor of the occasion. The trains were scheduled to leave daily on the thirty-six-hour trip. It would be only a matter of time before AT&SF service to Chicago would be inaugurated.[64]

These developments were quickly followed by another of equal importance. The Santa Fe and the Mallory steamship line announced an agreement to run steamers between New York and a connection with the Santa Fe at Galveston. According to the *Daily News,* "The special object of the arrangement with the steamship company is to carry freight from New York to the Pacific Coast via Galveston, making the Santa Fe independent of the eastern railroads on large consignments."[65] This was the first mention of an arrangement between the two transportation organizations, but it should be remembered that the Ball, Hutchings & Company partners, especially George Ball, were investors in the Mallory line and it is not surprising that the surviving partners, Sealy and John H. Hutchings, would have been instrumental in an agreement beneficial to the Santa Fe, the Mallory line, the Galveston Wharf Company, and the city of Galveston.[66]

This agreement—by far the largest land-sea networking arrangement thus far for Galveston—was of great significance at the time. The Atchison had rapidly grown into one of the nation's largest railroads as a result of its construction and acquisitions. The 5,349 miles owned at the end of 1886 were expanded by 501 more by the early part of 1887. President Strong estimated that the mileage would total 6,500 by the end of 1887, excluding the Chicago line under construction. When completed, that line would add another 450 miles, bringing the total to 7,000 miles, second only to the Pennsylvania system. And additional acquisition not yet announced would increase that figure. In describing the record of the AT&SF, the *Railway Age* said, "The career of this company has been one of the marvels of railway enterprise and it would be unsafe now to attempt to fix a limit to its expansion or to the ambitions of its Napoleonic president or its bold and enterprising directors; but that they will not rest content until sitting in their Boston offices they control by far the greatest aggregation of railway lines that the world has known is very evident."[67]

The capital stock of the Atchison company reached $64,893,250, which included an increase of $7,980,000 caused by the issuance of that amount in exchange for the stock of the Gulf, Colorado & Santa Fe. The bonded debt was $40,131,000, and, reported the *Railway Age*, "including other liabilities, this great company now represents a total investment of $145,032,444."[68]

The *Daily News* exclaimed that "the effect of the absorption of the Galveston road into the Atchison system has not been felt in any perceptible degree as yet, but the day is not far distant when great results to Galveston must follow therefrom. . . . The outlook for Galveston was never better than at the present time." The same editorial, perhaps with the benefit of knowledge of some behind-the-scenes discussions, urged both private and public authorities to adopt a liberal policy toward the Atchison's coming need for terminal facilities.[69]

As the Atchison continued to prosper after the acquisition of the Gulf, Colorado & Santa Fe, Jay Gould began to find his own fortunes declining. Beset by illness and debt, he began to see the pieces of his railroad empire slipping away, one by one. He abandoned his Mexican plans and left the field to General Palmer. The Atchison was providing stiff competition to the Kansas & Pacific across the plains, and also threatening the Missouri, Kansas & Texas, old and expensive to operate, on the route to the Gulf. On the California to New Orleans route, Huntington's Southern Pacific system was running the Texas & Pacific out of business. In another move to Galveston's benefit, the Katy broke away from Gould's grip and later signed a long-term agreement with the I&GN to share the Galveston, Houston & Henderson between Houston and Galveston. When Gould died in 1892, his estate had largely been reduced to his holdings in the Western Union Telegraph and Manhattan Elevated companies. Events left Galveston by 1890 with excellent railroad connections to all parts of the west, except California where Huntington was still holding out for deep water before building a terminal at Galveston with a direct line into the city.[70]

CHAPTER SEVEN

HUNTINGTON
LOOKS EASTWARD

Whereas Jay Gould wanted to own or control the Gulf, Colorado & Santa Fe Railway and sought a subsidy from Galveston to build terminal facilities, Collis P. Huntington was willing to bide his time waiting for deep water at Galveston while continuing to show interest throughout the 1880s. Huntington and his partners, Leland Stanford, Mark Hopkins, and Charles Crocker, became famous with the building of the first transcontinental railroad. They had built the Central Pacific from Sacramento over and through the Sierra Nevada to meet the Union Pacific at Promontory, Utah, on May 10, 1869. Then the Big Four, as the partners became known, combined the Central Pacific with the Southern Pacific and began building lines to the San Joaquin Valley and Los Angeles. The San Francisco to Los Angeles line was completed on September 5, 1876, beginning a long and often controversial period of domination of rail transportation in California.

But Huntington's plans extended far beyond the borders of California, or even the Pacific Coast. California's agricultural importance had grown to significant proportions by 1880, and the Southern Pacific had its eye on both eastern and European markets for California products. California's wheat production had passed 29 million bushels by 1880 and would increase to 40 million bushels by 1890, making the state second in wheat production behind Minnesota's 52 million. Huntington's goal was to have a port on the Gulf of Mexico to serve as a terminal for a land-sea network to the East Coast and Europe. With this goal in mind, he began to push the Southern Pacific eastward. Galveston was well aware of the plans and recognized that New Orleans, with its deeper harbor, held an advantage over the Texas port in spite of Galveston being 300 miles closer to California than was New Orleans. By 1877 the Southern Pacific had reached Yuma, Arizona, where Hopkins would die the following year. In 1878 the tracks reached Tucson, Arizona, and were extended to El Paso, Texas, on

May 19, 1881. At this point Huntington was poised to play a major role in the burgeoning Texas railroad scene.[1]

Huntington began by acquiring Colonel Tom Peirce's Galveston, Harrisburg & San Antonio on June 3, 1881, and announcing that the GH&SA would start building west to meet the Southern Pacific system coming east. This announcement was followed shortly by the news that he acquired the Texas & New Orleans (Houston to Orange) and the Louisiana Western (Orange to Vermillionville, Louisiana). The remaining 143 miles to New Orleans, covered by the Morgan Company line, would be the final link. Although the Morgan estate initially refused to sell the line to Huntington, it was soon reported that they had entered into an agreement known as the California-Pacific combination. Although Galveston held out hopes that some of the Pacific Coast traffic would find its way to its wharves, it was obvious that the lack of a deep water harbor was giving Huntington no other choice but to opt for terminal facilities at New Orleans.[2]

In an unusual move for the ordinarily tight-lipped business leaders of the day, Huntington published a statement of the intentions of the Southern Pacific. He cited the following as the reasons for the eastward expansion of the road: a short rail line between the Pacific Ocean and the Gulf of Mexico; service to the mining industries in the Mexican states of Sonora and Chihuahua; the desirability of a "Southern alternative" route between the Atlantic Coast and the Pacific; and a more direct union between the growing network of roads in Louisiana, Texas and Mexico with those of the Pacific Coast. The statement included an analysis of international trading patterns, pointing out that ships make triangular voyages via Australia to San Francisco because of insufficient return cargoes. The analysis also stated that in 1880 there was a surplus of 400,000 tons of wheat and equivalent flour left unshipped for which the available grain ships and inland transportation were inadequate. It concluded that the route with the shortest land carriage and a single inexpensive transfer at a Gulf port would have a decided advantage for certain higher classes of freights passing in either direction and westbound passengers.[3]

The statement next compared the relative advantages of the T&P, building across northern Texas to El Paso, with the proposed southern route through San Antonio and Houston. The southern route clearly passed through more settled country and possessed the advantage of lower and more equable grades. In addition, San Antonio was destined to become a great agricultural center and Houston was a railroad center of importance already. With the additional advantage of the anticipated connecting roads coming from Mexico, the southern route was shown to superior. If deep water harbors were to be achieved at the Texas ports, 300 miles closer to California than New Orleans, the advantage would be even greater.[4] Huntington's intentions, however, were obvious to Gould as early as June, 1881, when the Texas & Pacific filed a claim in the courts of Arizona and New Mexico that the Southern Pacific constructed its road through those states on the right-of-way granted the T&P in its charter of 1871 by Congress. The charter authorized the T&P to build westward on or near the thirty-second parallel to the Pacific Ocean and gave it a grant right-of-way 400 feet in width through government lands.[5]

Having taken the defensive measure in the courts to stop Huntington in Arizona and New Mexico, Gould took the offensive measure of planning a line from Ogden, Utah, into San Francisco, parallelling Huntington's Central Pacific. Gould intended to do this by extending a subsidiary of the Union Pacific to the Nevada-California border and buying control of a feeder line, the Nevada Central, to connect it to San Francisco. Gould even suggested to the Atchison, Topeka & Santa Fe, the Frisco, and the Atlantic & Pacific the forming of a coalition against Huntington's group. Faced with this double threat to his western empire, Huntington reacted boldly, using Gould's own weaponry—the parallel road. Huntington promptly announced that the Central Pacific, which had linked up with the Union Pacific in 1869 to form the first transcontinental line, would now build eastward parallelling the Union Pacific to Omaha.[6]

At this point, the two men, pragmatists that they were, decided a compromise that protected the true interests of each would better serve their purposes than would overextending themselves, and by early November rumors began to spread that a compromise had been reached. Details of the agreement began to leak out slowly, and finally the complete terms of the agreement were published. Because of the significance of the agreement at the time, the details merit some attention. The T&P and Southern Pacific system would intersect 80 miles east of El Paso at Sierra Blanca and both parties would share on equal terms the line to El Paso. At the other end of the line, the Southern Pacific would have the same access to the T&P eighty miles from New Orleans under the same equal terms. For the privilege of using the road into El Paso, and the perpetual privilege into Los Angeles, San Francisco, and San Diego on terms equal to the most favored user, the T&P relinquished its claim to the land grant right-of-way and franchises west of El Paso to the Southern Pacific company. The T&P agreed not to extend its road west of El Paso so long as the Southern Pacific complied with the agreement, and the Southern Pacific agreed not to build parallel lines to the T&P in Texas or to other Gould lines in Arkansas or Missouri. The agreement provided that, once the connection to New Orleans was completed, the seaboard business from

El Paso to New Orleans would be divided equally between the two lines and their connections. Although Huntington was bypassing Galveston for the moment, the agreement recognized the future potential of the Texas port by including it in the provisions. Since the two systems intersected at Houston, it provided that both roads would use the Galveston line, the GH&H, running through trains if necessary. It also provided that the though business to and from El Paso and the Pacific would be divided on the basis of one-third to the Texas & Pacific and its connections, and two-thirds to the line via San Antonio, since it was the shortest route.[7]

On December 1, 1881, at 4 P.M. the Texas & Pacific track met the Southern Pacific at Sierra Blanca, giving the nation its second Pacific connection over the long discussed "Southern Route" close to the 32nd parallel. Second only to the trackage laid by the Union Pacific, 505 miles of track had been laid by the Texas & Pacific since the resumption of work in April, 1880, with 425 miles of that coming in 1881. Managing the effort were two of the nation's top railroad executives, General Grenville Dodge, head of the construction company, and Herbert M. Hoxie, Gould's general manager of the Texas & Pacific. Dodge had also managed the building of the Union Pacific, and Hoxie was one of his top engineers. The effort of the Southern Pacific was equally prodigious, having completed 373 miles across Arizona, 182 in New Mexico, and over 100 miles in Texas. The line building west from San Antonio reached Uvalde on November 20, 1881, and had since progressed across the Nueces River heading toward Spofford, where a branch was being built to Eagle Pass to meet a planned road from Mexico City. With the California to New Orleans connection via the Texas & Pacific now complete, and with the completion of the Huntington line through San Antonio now in sight, the full impact of Galveston's loss of trade to New Orleans really began to sink in. The Gould and Huntington plans were now a reality, and three years of futile efforts had passed for Galveston without the first step being taken toward the achievement of deep water.[8]

Having pledged not to build competing lines against each other, Gould and Huntington next moved against a common enemy—the St. Louis & San Francisco, or Frisco—with consequences for Galveston. With their acquisition of a controlling interest, Gould and Huntington immediately announced that the Frisco would abandon plans to link with the Atlantic and Pacific in a transcontinental route to California across the 35th parallel. They also announced that the route across the Indian Territory, parallel to Gould's MKT to Denison, would be stopped. With the purchase Huntington maintained his monopoly on connections to California and Gould maintained his monopoly on Texas connections to St. Louis. Galveston interests had seen the Frisco line to Paris as an outlet to St. Louis for the GC&SF, using the Chicago, Texas & Mexican connection from Cleburne to Paris. Gould's move cut off possibilities for these two roads to reach the East. In addition, the move cut off the Houston & Texas Central from going ahead with its plans for a line from Ennis to Paris. While the curtailment of the Frisco plans might prove to be of benefit to the Gulf ports looking to the Pacific trade coming over the Southern Pacific, the state of Texas as a whole was sure to lose as a result of the lack of competition on the roads to St. Louis. The Gould move was described as one "entirely worthy of the Napoleon of railroad tactics."[9] The purported acquisition by Gould and Huntington also began to increase the volume of the cries against monopoly, especially in regard to Texas, since Gould's Missouri Pacific included the Katy and the Iron Mountain, from Denison and Texarkana respectively, where rates were reported to have increased ten cents per hundred pounds already.[10] In spite of the problems for the state at large, the Galveston business interests were able to take heart when the GH&H announced that an agreement had been reached that would enable the Southern Pacific to run trains from San Francisco into Galveston on a regular basis as soon as the connections were complete between El Paso and San Antonio.[11]

HUNTINGTON'S FIRST VISIT

March 21, 1882, became one of the significant milestones in Galveston's economic development when Huntington visited the island for the first time. In spite of the recent developments regarding access to and facilities in New Orleans, Huntington left no doubt as to his future hopes for Galveston as a great port once 25 feet of water was obtained over the bar. He fixed on 25 feet after discussions with leading shipping interests led him to believe that 8,000-ton ships requiring 25 feet were most fitting for sea business. Accompanied by Thomas W. Peirce, the president of the GH&SA, he visited the Cotton Exchange, Colonel Mansfield's Army Engineers office, the Strand, the site of the harbor works, and the beach during their three-hour visit. Among those who visited with him were Moritz Kopperl, Leon Blum, Julius Kaufman, and Julius Runge. Having made his arrangement with the GH&H for access to the island, Huntington made it abundantly clear that the next move was up to Galveston. "You must have twenty-five feet of water on your bar—do not stop at twenty feet," he warned. He added, perhaps with more understanding than he was aware of, that perhaps the channel between the jetties should be narrowed.

Not much time during the visit was devoted to railroad affairs, but part of the interview dealt with railroad politics. Like Gould before him, he stopped in Austin, spent an hour with Governor Oran Roberts, and was pleased with the head of Texas affairs. Huntington favored laws preventing discrimination but thought attempts to regulate freights by legislative action would lead to disaster. He expressed his hope of completing the San Francisco to Galveston and New Orleans line by September, and revealed his plans to improve the quality of the GH&SA roadbed and trackage in order that it could carry the heavy tonnage that he expected after the line opened.[12]

Huntington left Galveston without any announcements or indications of any specific moves on his part. However, by July the rumors had begun to fly. First, it was reported that Gould and Huntington were negotiating with Charles Whitney, the president of the Morgan interests, to purchase the H&TC. This was quickly followed by rumors that the H&TC had already surveyed the land and bay around Virginia Point and that three dredge boats were now being ordered up to cut a channel to Virginia Point. The plan here was that, having been shut out of facilities on the island itself, Gould and Huntington would build wharf facilities at Virginia Point to reach the channel, and an extension would be built from the GH&H to the wharves. It was recognized that while such a move might not be to the benefit of all interests in Galveston, it would be in the greater interests of both Galveston and the state to have such an enlargement and cheapening of port facilities. In addition, the solution to the problem of the 25-foot channel to the Gulf would then become of vital interest to the Gould-Huntington faction. The rumors may have been nothing more than another negotiating ploy by the Gould and Huntington people to strengthen their hand, since nothing materialized.[13]

The expected connection of the Southern Pacific with the GH&SA did not occur in 1882 as planned, but other events of importance to Texas and Galveston involving Gould and Huntington did happen. First, on August 2, President Chester Arthur signed the act giving the St. Louis & San Francisco Railway Company the right of way through the Indian Territory from Fort Smith, Arkansas, to a point near Paris, Texas. In spite of the rumors about Huntington and Gould gaining control earlier in the year, it was now obvious that they had not and the plans of the Frisco to build parallel to Gould's Katy were proceeding in spite of his opposition. Not only did the bill break the Gould hold on the Texas-St. Louis traffic, it also established for the first time that the right of eminent domain lodged with Congress was equally applicable to the Indian Territory. This historical milestone played an important role in shaping the futures of both the Indian Territory—the eventual state of Oklahoma—and Texas. From Paris the Frisco would reach into all parts of Texas through its connection to the Texas and Pacific and to the two non-Gould roads—the H&TC and the GC&SF. By December, Frisco officials announced their building plans for the 160-mile road from Van Buren, Arkansas, to the Golden Bluff on the Red River where a bridge would be built.[14] The second bit of startling news affecting the state was created by Huntington when three of his roads—the GH&SA, the T&NO, and the Louisiana Western—issued a circular announcing they would no longer accept through bills of lading issued by the Gould roads. The move was only the first step by Huntington in a strategy of ignoring certain parts of the agreement of November, 1881, that would eventually lead to serious financial troubles on the part of the Texas & Pacific.[15]

In 1883 Huntington completed his California to New Orleans line. On January 12, the Southern Pacific building east and the GH&SA building west met at the Pecos River, where the silver spike was driven. On February 6, the first train from New Orleans reached San Antonio, and on February 7, the first train from Los Angeles reached there. Next Huntington announced his purchase of Morgan's Louisiana & Texas Railroad and Steamship Company (the sea-rail network built and operated so successfully by Charles Morgan until his death) for $7,500,000, or $150 per share. This purchase gave Huntington the Vermillionville-New Orleans connection for his railroad, the Morgan fleet of ships, and a controlling interest of 400,000 shares of stock in the H&TC railroad with its Texas Central branch running northwest from Waco and its connection to Paris under construction. The acquisition was soon followed by reports that all ships would be taken off the New Orleans to Galveston run. Instead, freight would be hauled from New Orleans by rail to Clinton and then by ship to the ports of the Western Gulf. This news was quickly followed by rumors that the GC&SF was negotiating with the Southern Pacific to use Galveston as the port instead of Clinton with the GC&SF serving the Southern Pacific's interests and providing terminal facilities at its property at the east end of the harbor.[16]

These negotiations did not produce results, and the matter of Virginia Point arose again with the report that the Huntington interests had made a conditional purchase of a tract of land there. Again, without being specific, local interests made reference to the opposition. It may have been the partners of the Ball, Hutchings Company who dominated the GC&SF directory and the Wharf Company, who were creating obstacles for the entry of the Southern Pacific; however, eventually it would be George Sealy who would play the largest role in bringing Southern Pacific facilities to the Island. Again, the "conditional" purchase may have been only another tactic employed by Huntington to force better terms. By October it was revealed that Huntington had taken a lease on the Galveston Flats, an area west of the Wharf Company waterfront property. No terms were revealed, and nothing was said about the demise of the opposition. The move was looked upon as proof that Huntington was earnest in his attempt to make Galveston the grand terminal of his Southern Pacific system, even to the extent that his company would dredge a deep water channel to the Gulf when it finally appeared that all other means had failed.[17]

HUNTINGTON RETURNS

In the spring of 1884 Huntington was back again, staying overnight at the Beach Hotel and receiving courtesy calls from prominent citizens and leading business men. Although he was not available for interview, it was reported that he advised the Galvestonians to go for the Eads Bill, a separate appropriation for deep water, if that was what they wanted, and not to accept anything less. No business discussions were reported, as usual, but again it is likely that limited talks took place.[18]

Huntington's involvement with Galveston was carried a step further in September when the Southern Pacific leased additional wharfage and warehouse facilities in order to use the port for transferring freights brought by Huntington ships from New York bound for the interior. The freight would be carried to Houston using the GH&H rights Huntington had obtained in November, 1881, to connections with the H&TC and the GH&SA of the Southern Pacific system. This development left Galveston with a double line of steamers from Galveston to New York, such as it had once been before Morgan pulled out of Galveston and began to use Clinton as his port.[19]

In the meantime Huntington had incorporated the Southern Pacific in Kentucky on March 17, 1884, and completed the transcontinental network of roads under his management or ownership, becoming the first to do so. While purchasing and building the Southern Pacific system from San Francisco to New Orleans, Huntington was also extending the Chesapeake and Ohio to Memphis. This provided a connection of 1,120 miles between Memphis and Newport News. The 455-mile gap between Memphis and New Orleans was closed by consolidating four roads—the Tennessee Southern, the New Orleans & Baton Rouge, the Vicksburg & Memphis, and the New Orleans & Mississippi Valley—into a single new line, the Louisville, New Orleans & Texas. With this transaction completed, the Huntington line stretched 4,070 miles from San Francisco to Newport News and brought him further national acclaim.[20]

In spite of these accomplishments, the slowdown in business across the nation was affecting Huntington and his roads as well as everyone else. With the end of 1884 the emphasis would shift from expansion to holding on. By 1885 the fates of the Gould and Huntington systems in Texas and the GC&SF would be bound together by the lengthy negotiations for shares of a dwindling market.

CHAPTER EIGHT

THE SOUTHERN PACIFIC COMES TO GALVESTON

The construction of the Southern Pacific terminal and wharf facilities came as a fitting climax to Galveston's thirty-five-year effort to become "the seaport of the Great West." With SP president Collis P. Huntington's agreement of January 11, 1899, to create facilities equal to or better than those he had built at Algiers, across the Mississippi River from New Orleans, he would soon be able to transfer cargoes from Southern Pacific boxcars to Southern Pacific (Morgan Line) ships 361 miles closer than Algiers. Products from the entire West Coast, especially California wheat, would now move through Galveston at Southern Pacific's piers A and B.

The move to Galveston, which began with rumors in 1878 and was furthered with Huntington's visits to the city in the early 1880s, seemed a long time coming. Huntington's basic requirement for the port was a deep water channel capable of handling ships drawing 24–25 feet. He supported the efforts of the deep water committee through the remainder of the 1880s until President Benjamin Harrison signed the bill on September 19, 1890, that guaranteed the Army Corps of Engineers $6,200,00 to build the twin jetties that would provide the deep water channel to the Gulf of Mexico.

With deep water achieved in 1896, the SP was ready to make its move. However, as was the case with the 1890 Deep Water Bill, the final thrust to implement the decision was hampered by circumstances. Four separate problems occurred and had to be resolved before construction could actually begin:

1. The SP and the Galveston City Company, owner of the property, had to negotiate a price for the vacant land (city blocks 700–710) along the north shore of the island sought by Huntington.

2. A group of Galveston businessmen, incorporated as the West End Dock Company, had obtained a permit from the Army Corps of Engineers and Secretary of War R. A. Alger to dig a channel through

the flats to the main harbor channel in front of the same area sought by Huntington. Thus, they claimed rights to the flats.

3. The Galveston City Council, recognizing state ownership of the flats, had contracted with attorney Leo N. Levi to seek a title grant from the state enabling the city to develop wharfage facilities on the flats in front of city blocks 700 – 710.

4. The Galveston City Council had to grant permission for any owner of blocks 700 – 710 to close Avenue B in front of the property and the side streets (Forty-first through Fiftieth Streets) so that an owner, such as the Southern Pacific, would have a single piece of property with free access for railroad tracks.

The property of the Galveston Wharf Company stopped at Forty-first Street (block 699) and therefore was not a party to these entanglements, although it had had similar problems with the ownership of the flats (the very shallow water between the shoreline and the deep channel) earlier in its history. Therefore, George Sealy, who became president of the Wharf Company in February, 1898, was free to act as an intermediary for Huntington with Galveston City Company president John H. Hutchings, who was also Sealy's partner in the Hutchings Sealy Bank.

HUNTINGTON'S NEGOTIATIONS

The years of speculation about Huntington's interest in and plans for terminal facilities at Galveston were ended May 11, 1896, when Alexander C. Hutchinson, the president of the Atlantic System of the Southern Pacific line, which included the Morgan Steamship Line, came to Galveston. The deep water channel was nearing 24 feet and Hutchinson now made it clear that the Southern Pacific would come if all of their requirements for space were met. Initially, however, the negotiations were between the SP and the Galveston Wharf Company for the use of existing facilities. When Hutchinson left Galveston, he had a proposal from the Wharf Company for analysis. As he left he remarked that the company's analysis would have to find that the volume of trade passing over the wharves would be profitable after the Wharf Company's charges were paid.[1]

Another important event happened the same day that Hutchinson departed. The Galveston, La Porte & Houston railroad (Galveston's fifth railroad) entered the city over its own bridge (the fourth bridge over the bay at Virginia Point). Regular rail service to Houston via La Porte was thus inaugurated on a daily basis. This railroad, which was already in receivership, resulted from the merger of the La Porte, Houston & Northern with the North Galveston, Houston & Kansas City. As the negotiations progressed, the Southern Pacific, presently using the Gulf, Colorado & Santa Fe and the Galveston, Houston & Henderson tracks to enter Galveston, became interested in having its own line into the city and eventually purchased the La Porte.[2]

Although Hutchinson's visit marked only the opening of lengthy negotiations, the press saw it as a momentous occasion, the first achievement resulting from deep water. "The Southern Pacific system, with its vast marine and railroad traffic covering the great west and Mexico, is the crowning event. Its coming places Galveston in command of an increased traffic large enough to insure commercial prosperity," stated the *Galveston Daily News.* And the joy in Galveston was equaled by the gloom in New Orleans where it was fully recognized that every positive for Galveston was a negative for the Crescent City. In a long dispatch from New Orleans, it was reported that there was much concern there about recent events that may have contributed to the SP decision. It was known that Morgan line ships were leaving with partial cargoes and that ships had been laid up during cotton's dull season. There also was a recent decision by arbitrators in the cotton insurance differential problem that SP officials were openly dissatisfied with. These factors, plus Galveston's 361-mile advantage for the SP, were economic issues that the company could not ignore. The businessmen of New Orleans accepted them as the facts of life in a changing business world.[3]

The negotiations between the parties went underground until Huntington himself visited Galveston on March 26, 1898. This time the news of his visit was pushed to the back pages by the news of the preparation for the coming war with Spain and the increase of the fortifications around Galveston Island and Bolivar Peninsula. Several subjects were covered in the interview with Huntington, including his opinion that the explosion of the battleship *Maine* was not a cause for war. He described his trip as his annual inspection of facilities and said he came to Galveston because of the large quantities of freight being transferred from rail to ship and from ship to rail. As far as SP terminal facilities, he said that there were no immediate prospects. "When we come to Galveston we want to come right, and on a large scale," he said, indicating that the Galveston Wharf Company offer was inadequate. Much of the interview was devoted to discussion of his plans to buy the Galveston, La Porte & Houston railroad. He had hoped to come to Galveston over his own tracks, but the condition of the road required closer inspection before a bid would be submitted.[4]

The status of the negotiations were made clear in a long letter to Sealy that Huntington sent while en route to San Francisco. Not much was agreed upon yet. He made his basic position clear: "The Southern Pacific Company would not care to do business in Galveston unless it could be in shape there to handle the greatest possible volume which it could fetch and carry." He explained that he envisioned products from Oregon and California going to Europe by way of Galveston, and copper and other metals from northern New Mexico moving through the Gulf to their destinations.[5]

He went on to state the SP's requirements specifically:

1. 3700 feet of water frontage, starting at 41st street.

2. Piers 1200 feet in length would require 1800 feet from the head of the pier running back to allow space for the transfer of cargo between ship and rail.

3. Gift or lease of this land by the city, City Company and state for 99 years, in recognition of the fact that dredging the channel and slips, and filling in behind the bulkheads will be very expensive.

As for the potential legal entanglements, Huntington suggested that the parties go ahead so work could start, with the understanding all would comply with any title decisions or court decisions that might follow.

Since Huntington mentioned the City Company instead of the Galveston Wharf Company, apparently it had been decided that the Wharf Company could not provide enough space for the SP. Thus, in the next paragraph from his letter, he seems to seek Sealy's influence in negotiating with the City Company: "In writing you as above, I do not forget that you are a member of the Wharf Company, but I have no hesitation in asking you to help us secure what we will require, because I know quite well that Mr. Seely [sic] desires first of all the welfare and advancement of the City of Galveston, and because I also know that whatever our companies would do there in the way of making great improvements and creating new facilities for commerce, would redound far more to the prosperity of Galveston than it possibly could to our own interest.[6] Shortly afterwards Sealy must have initiated efforts on Huntington's behalf because he obtained a precise map of the West End flats from attorney Eugene A. Hawkins, the agent for the City Company, and forwarded it to Huntington.[7]

In August the *Galveston Tribune*, perhaps concerned with the progress of the negotiations, issued a warning to the parties involved that Huntington was not without options as far as Galveston was concerned. Reminding readers that since Huntington had already built port facilities at San Francisco; Algiers, Louisiana; and Newport News, Virginia, it would be little trouble for him to proceed with plans for development of Virginia Point (the mainland opposite Galveston Island). The article also claimed that Huntington was now the real owner of the Galveston, La Porte & Houston Railroad connecting Virginia Point to Houston and the other Southern Pacific lines.[8]

Virginia Point had been the subject of stories connecting it with Huntington since his trips to Galveston in the early 1880s. As it was, these stories were much more than rumors, although the facts never seemed to be made public. References were made to Huntington's plans for the mainland adjacent to Galveston as if they were only in the talking stage.[9] As a matter of fact, Huntington had actually signed an option-to-buy contract with landowner Judge William J. Jones for a sizable plot adjacent to the GH&H railroad tracks and filed a plat with the county clerk's office. The first agreement between the parties was signed August 8, 1883, followed by a supplement agreement of the same date, and an indenture signed December 10, 1883. In 1891 another contract was prepared but was not signed.[10]

These documents provided that Huntington would pay Judge Jones $250 per year and that Jones could continue to occupy the land. In the event that Huntington had not spent at least $100,000 within ten years on improvements to the tract of land described, the property would revert to Jones. A total sale price for the land was never stated, so it reads like an "option to buy" arrangement. Perhaps it was only a means of achieving just what it did—frequent discussion in the press of the options open to Huntington if deep water became available.[11]

Three articles in October, 1883, openly discussed all of the factors that would affect Huntington's choice between Virginia Point and Galveston and stressed the need for all parties involved with the economic future of the port, especially those working for deep water, to press ahead and to create the conditions that would bring the Southern Pacific terminal facilities. Perhaps everyone took some comfort when it was finally announced that Huntington had leased wharf and warehouse facilities from the Galveston Wharf Company, and that the GH&H railroad would provide the connection between Galveston and the Huntington railroads at Houston—the Houston & Texas Central and the Galveston, Harrisburg & San Antonio. Surely Huntington was serious about facilities on Galveston Island instead of the mainland. These arrangements probably continued until 1896, when Hutchinson came to Galveston to negotiate with Sealy about more space from the Galveston Wharf Company.[12]

However, Huntington was not yet finished. In March, 1885, a bill was introduced in the Texas Legislature granting the flats in front of Judge Jones's Virginia Point tract to him, in order that he could include the flats if he sold the property. Of course, the flats would be needed if wharves were to be built and a channel dug out to the main channel of Galveston harbor. This same problem existed all around the shores of Galveston Bay. Knowing that Huntington still had his eye on the mainland, in spite of his agreement with the Wharf Company for island facilities, would serve to keep the commercial interests in Galveston aware of the need to accommodate the Southern Pacific's needs or lose them.[13]

It therefore was not surprising that the matter of Virginia Point was raised again in August, 1898, with the added factor that the Galveston, La Porte & Houston Railroad was a reality, and it would connect in Houston with the Huntington system's coast-to-coast rail network. With negotiations now coming to a head as a result of Sealy's involvement, the Galveston City Council issued a formal invitation on October 8, 1898, for Huntington and the Southern Pacific to come to Galveston. On October 10 word came that Huntington could be expected in Galveston in two months; on October 15 word came that he was pleased. On October 20, the City Company made a firm offer to sell for $150,000, half of the original asking price but more than Huntington's $100,000 reply. Then like a lightning bolt, on October 22 came news from New York: "We do not want the property."[14]

Records do not reveal what got the negotiations back on track, but the next month, Huntington wrote to Agent Hawkins requesting that the City Company send someone with authority to New York to work out the remaining disagreements between the parties. Hawkins was named, and he arrived in New York in late November to resolve the final questions with Huntington and his attorney, Charles H. Tweed—questions pertaining to proper titles to the property as well as price. Perhaps another negotiating ploy was introduced when Hawkins was made aware by Huntington's private secretary that Huntington had opposition within the company, and difficult terms on the purchase would make it that much harder for him.[15]

By December 8, 1898, Hawkins was able to inform President Hutchings that they were close to settlement and that Tweed was to present him the draft of a contract the next day. The last points that Huntington insisted upon were delaying construction until all claimants had relinquished rights to the company and not specifying any fixed amounts for improvements, saying only that he would develop terminals. The following day, Hawkins forwarded the draft contract to Hutchings, stating that he was still trying to change some conditions that did not conform to the resolutions passed by the board of the City Company.

The results of these additional efforts were passed on to Hutchings on December 14. The following day Hawkins notified Huntington that the contract had been sent to Galveston and the board had objected to several provisions: Closing Avenue B making other City Company property inaccessible, no fixed time for the acceptance of the property and examination of the title, and the postponement of the expenditure of $150,000 for improvements until all legal issues were resolved.[16]

Negotiations may have stopped over the Christmas holidays, although there was much compromising to be done between the two parties. Nevertheless, the *Galveston Daily News* was brimming with optimism on January 1, 1899, when it devoted two full columns to Huntington and the Southern Pacific, stating that the deal between the Galveston City Company and Huntington was "now to be expected at any moment" and that the achievement of the 28-foot depth in the channel made it possible.

And so it was. The agreement was signed on January 11, 1899, and a price of $200,000, payable in four timed installments, was established. Huntington agreed to spend $150,000 within two years for dredging, piers, and terminal facilities, and, of course, there was a contingency clause regarding the relinquishing of rights by the city and the state. The main issue was now resolved, but there were others.[17]

THE WEST END DOCK COMPANY

While the Huntington interests were still negotiating with the Galveston Wharf Company in 1897, a group of Galveston businessmen in May of that year organized the West End Dock Company. On July 19, they requested permission from the Army Corps of Engineers, responsible for all of the harbor activities, for permission to dig a channel through the West End flats to connect with the main harbor channel. Directors of the company were G. H. Mensing, Gustave Reymershoffer, T. William English, V. E. Austin, Joseph Lobit, I. H. Kempner, T. J. Groce, Walter Gresham, George E. Mann, and John D. Rogers. The request resulted in a study report on expansion of the harbor by Colonel Henry Robert, the chief of the Engineers southwestern district, who had also been involved in the very important study of Galveston a decade earlier. He concluded that expansion of the harbor was an absolute necessity for future growth and for receiving the maximum benefit from the jetties just constructed by the Engineers.

On December 11, 1897, Secretary of War R. A. Alger, acting upon Robert's recommendation, gave the West End Dock Company permission to dig the channel. A conflict now arose between the West End Dock Company and the City Company, which claimed rights to the flats, and

the city, which maintained that the rights belonged to the state and accused the West End Dock Company of "attempting to secure for private
purposes a large area of public domain that should belong to the city for
future port development."[18]

That situation remained unresolved until October, 1898, when the city
council issued the invitation to Huntington to come to Galveston. Following that meeting a committee was formed consisting of three council
members, three representatives of the City Company, and three representatives of the West End Dock Company for the purpose of working out
Huntington's entry. It was said that "a patriotic spirit would prevail." As
public pressure rose in support of Huntington, patriotic spirit did prevail;
the West End Dock Company relinquished its claim and the City Company agreed to the city asking the state for ownership rights.[19]

THE LEVI CONTRACT

The third obstacle requiring clearance for the Huntington sale to proceed was the city's contract with Leo N. Levi. Following Colonel Robert's
report in October, 1897, Levi, an attorney, appeared before city council on
November 2, 1897, to advise the council that the flats were state property
and recommend that the city apply for a state grant of those flats for the
purpose of building harbor facilities. The advice was taken under consideration, and on January 18, 1898, the council contracted with Levi that, in
return for his obtaining the flats for the city, the council would award him
a lease for forty years of 10 percent of the waterfront facing the flats, to be
picked by him, for wharf or terminal use. Once Huntington quit his negotiations with the Wharf Company for more space in August, 1898, and
began to talk to the City Company about city blocks 700–710, the property adjoining the flats, it was obvious that there was now a serious problem of claims and rights that would be difficult to solve. Once the contract
between Huntington and the City Company was signed, the Southern
Pacific stated that the Levi contract was totally objectionable, and the city
council was left with no alternative but to abrogate the contract.[20]

CITY AND STATE PERMISSIONS

Once the city council had issued its formal invitation to Huntington
on October 8, 1898, the council was bound to pursue whatever course
was necessary to remove any obstacles, such as closing city streets in the

tract in question, and to seek from the state the rights over the flats in front of blocks 700–710. On February 3, 1899, a mass meeting was held, and a large number of interested citizens signed a petition to the council. The council acted quickly, passing an ordinance on February 6 recognizing the purchase by the Southern Pacific and granting permission to close the streets between Forty-first and Fifty-first and from Avenue B north to the channel, with the right to dredge and erect piers on the property. Next the council had the local representatives in the legislature present a bill confirming the city ordinance and ceding any state rights to the flats. The bill encountered a lot of opposition, inheriting some of the traditional opposition to the Galveston Wharf Company, but it survived and passed May 1, 1899. The last obstacle was cleared, and Huntington was completely free to come to Galveston. The city had another great achievement to celebrate, and the joy almost equaled that experienced at the passing of the Galveston deep water appropriation in 1890. There was nothing left to do but welcome Huntington, and Colonel Moody, as president of the Cotton Exchange, extended the invitation. Unfortunately, Huntington said that his heavy business schedule would not permit his acceptance at the time.[21]

HUNTINGTON COMES TO THE ISLAND

The people of Galveston had to wait almost a year to welcome and thank Huntington and his senior managers; they arrived March 15, 1900, traveling upon a train of five special cars. Those in the party included his wife, Arabella; his nephew and successor, Henry E. Huntington, who was vice president of the Southern Pacific; Julius Kruttschnitt, general manager of the Pacific Lines; William Hood, chief engineer of the Southern Pacific company; William Miles, private secretary to the president; and W. W. Kent, general manager of the Galveston, Houston & Northern, which purchased the Galveston, LaPorte & Houston in 1899. At this point in his life "the man in the black skull cap" had outlived all of his original partners—Leland Stanford, Mark Hopkins, and Charles Crocker—the Big Four, who had built the Central Pacific from Sacramento to Promontory, Utah, to meet the Union Pacific on May 10, 1869. There Stanford drove the famous "Golden Spike." And of course, no one suspected that this remarkable visitor was now nearing the end of the final year of his life.[22]

A welcoming party of John H. Hutchings, Judge George E. Mann, Joseph Clarke, Walter Gresham (who knew Huntington from the days of the Deep Water Committee), Marx Marx, Charles Clarke, John D. Rogers, John Adriance, George M. Courts, Dan B. Henderson, Leon Blum, Bertrand Adoue, Eugene A. Hawkins, and Judge William B. Lockhart boarded the cars to greet the visitors. They were followed by the local Southern Pacific personnel and a reporter from the *News,* whom Huntington thanked for being on time, remarking that "the newspaper boys call on me at all times; they even come out to my home [Fifth Avenue at 57th Street] at 11 o'clock at night, after I have retired." Huntington informed the reporter that the Southern Pacific would press ahead diligently and that their ships would be taking cotton over their piers by the end of the year. It was also pointed out that Huntington had finally reached his goal of coming to Galveston on his own train (the Houston East & West Texas), and he noted the good condition of the tracks and ties. The conversation shifted to manufacturing facilities; Huntington's opinions regarding the need for them and port facilities did not take his listeners by surprise. For ten years the business community had tried to encourage growth in this area, but so far cottonseed oil milling and flour milling had been the chief achievements. Huntington related that he once attempted to buy cotton fabric and was told that it cost $270 a pound, made from very fine cotton worth perhaps fifteen cents per pound. He felt that the port cities were missing a good bet by not converting the cotton into fabric. Other members of the party were also available for interviews. Kruttschnitt stated that the pier under construction would undoubtedly be "the finest in the United States."[23]

The chamber of commerce banquet honoring Huntington and his party was held at the Tremont House hotel March 16, with a large number of the members present. Also present for the dinner was the other dominant figure in the western railroad scene, Aldace F. Walker, president of the Atchison, Topeka & Santa Fe. Huntington gave a long speech in opposition to the Nicaraguan canal and to a Panama canal, which was getting some attention as an alternative. He gave a summary of the history of transportation in the United States, explaining how the people of New York would be foolish to appropriate $60,000,000 to resuscitate the Erie Canal, a relic rendered obsolete by the railroads. He pointed out that the private financiers had failed for fifty years to attempt construction because they knew the canal would be a financial failure. Revenues from the canal could never match the combined cost of interest, operations, and maintenance. Therefore, he said, it made no sense in 1898 for government to attempt what private business had rejected since 1850 as unprofitable. The advent of transcontinental railroads, including the Southern Pacific, had made the rails even more competitive by continually reducing their costs. Now, said

Huntington, with Galveston as the eastern terminus of the Southern Pacific, he was able to combine the best of both systems for quicker, cheaper movement of goods from coast to coast.[24]

Judge George E. Mann, Eugene A. Hawkins, and Walter Gresham gave toasts following Huntington's speech, elaborating on the significance of his plans for Galveston's harbor. Judge Mann described Huntington's system of linking rail and sea transportation as a method of seeking the lowest possible "cost of movement." He mentioned how Huntington explained his approach before a senate committee, indicating that his system could make a small profit at a rate that would bankrupt the railroads on transcontinental hauls. "He creates," said Mann, "a volume of freight more than double that which comes now to Galveston from all sources." The four great railroad systems—the Atchison, Topeka & Santa Fe; the Missouri, Kansas & Texas; Gould's I&GN; and the Southern Pacific—would become Galveston systems. Mann said a large portion of the freight in and out of the port must have the benefit of cheaper water transportation when competing with the Southern Pacific. In other words, the tracks must lead to the sea.[25]

Hawkins, who conducted the negotiations with Huntington on behalf of the Galveston City Company, reviewed the rise of Galveston as a port and cited the natural advantages that gave it a start. He mentioned how these advantages had been recognized by Stephen F. Austin in 1824, thirteen years before Michael B. Menard founded the city and the Galveston City Company. On behalf of the directors of the City Company he extended invitations to other companies interested in facilities at Galveston and assured them they would receive the same inducements and privileges accorded the Southern Pacific.[26]

In his speech, Gresham looked to the twentieth century when American shipping and commerce would reach around the world, continuing the history of the contributions of commerce to progress. He cited the large amounts of money being spent to improve harbors at Liverpool, Glasgow, Hamburg, and other ports as a sign that the expensiveness of modern ships required that harbors be built to serve the ships.

"If this city is to have the commercial greatness its geographical position and railway systems entitle it we must see that our harbor and railway facilities are improved and extended upon plans commensurate with the needs of commerce," he warned. He advised a policy of the removal of restrictions upon commerce and transportation. "With such a policy the twentieth century will see Texas the home of millions of prosperous and happy freemen, and Galveston the great emporium of the gulf," he concluded.[27]

Huntington's speech was not the end of his activities. Before leaving he bought the old Southern Compress property from H. M. Trueheart and Company for $112,500. This real estate was not adjacent to the large purchase, being located between Twenty-ninth and Thirty-second Streets on the east and west, and Postoffice and Church Streets on the north and south. The Galveston, La Porte & Houston railroad had acquired this property four years earlier, and the Galveston, Houston & Northern acquired it from the La Porte road. Another piece of land west of the city was purchased for right-of-way purposes for $10,000, making Huntington's total investment in property $322,500. The Southern Pacific would soon spend more than $2,000,000 on improvements.[28]

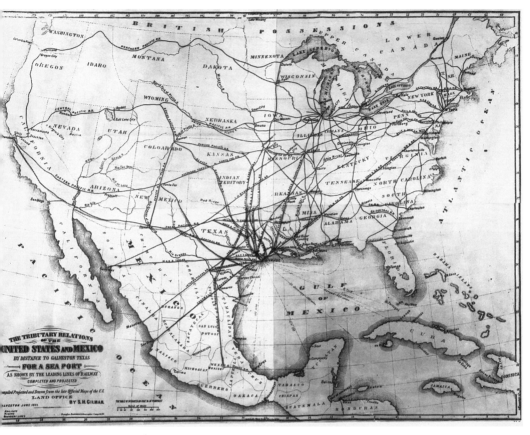

Captain S. H. Gilman's map depicts the railroad boom of 1871 when sixteen lines were chartered or planned to connect the port of Galveston to points to the east, west, and north. By 1900 five major roads had been built.

Courtesy Rosenberg Library

George Sealy.
Courtesy Kansas State Historical Society

Collis P. Huntington.
Courtesy Kansas State Historical Society

William B. Strong.
Courtesy Kansas State Historical Society

Jay Gould.
Courtesy Kansas State Historical Society

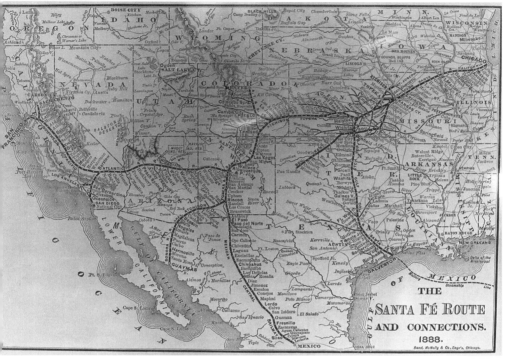

This 1888 map shows the Gulf, Colorado, and Santa Fe after it became a subsidiary of the Atchison, Topeka, and Santa Fe, providing an outlet to the Gulf of Mexico for that vast system. The AT&SF joined Galveston to a network with connections to Chicago in the east and San Francisco and Los Angeles in the west. Included in the system were Kansas City, Denver, and Albuquerque.

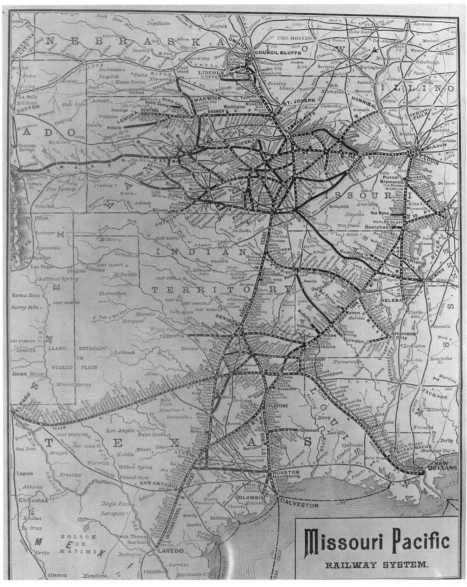

This 1888 map of Jay Gould's Missouri Pacific system and its several subsidiaries shows the network of railroads connecting Galveston to Omaha, Kansas City, and St. Louis. The Galveston, Houston, and Henderson provided the connection between Galveston and Houston; the International and Great Northern was the connection to Palestine; the St. Louis and Iron Mountain was the connection to St. Louis; and the Missouri, Kansas, and Texas was the connection to Kansas City.

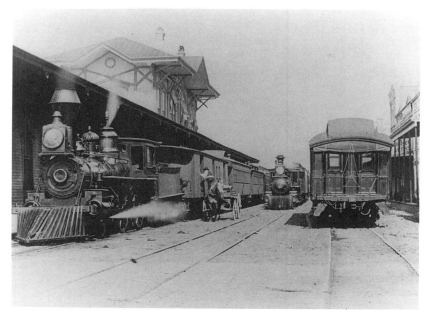

The Gulf, Colorado, and Santa Fe's first passenger terminal, completed in April, 1876, and used until September, 1897. The station was located on the north side of Avenue A, a short distance west of Twenty-third Street.
Courtesy Rosenberg Library

The Gulf, Colorado, and Santa Fe's Engine No. 93, a 4-4-0 type locomotive. Four small wheels are located in front on the truck and four large wheels are located on the main body of the engine. According to Nils Huxtable, in his book Classic North American Steam, *the 4-4-0 was the predominant engine on the North American continent, and 25,000 of them had been manufactured by 1900 by such companies as Rogers, Cooke, Baldwin, and Mason.*
Courtesy Rosenberg Library

Albert Somerville.
Courtesy Rosenberg Library

Moritz Kopperl.
Courtesy Rosenberg Library

General Braxton Bragg.
Courtesy Kansas State Historical Society

J. P. Fresenius.
Courtesy Kansas State Historical Society

Henry Rosenberg.
Courtesy Kansas State Historical Society

John Sealy.
Courtesy Kansas State Historical Society

The period of railroad history covered in this book, 1866–1990, has been described as the most prolific in history, when railroads made a vast territory in the western United States accessible in a very short time. Nowhere was this more true than in the vast expanses of Texas, where tracks were laid from end to end, mostly during the 1880s. In many cases these roads were built well in advance of settlement, and quick profitability was often impossible. Early investors in these railroads frequently lost all or much of their investments, particularly in years when poor crops turned marginal profits into hefty losses. Overburdened with debt, many of these companies were sold at prices far less than their construction costs. Then new owners stepped in to pick up the bargains and to operate the roads on a sounder financial basis.

Jay Gould was able to step in and buy the Texas & Pacific after Thomas A. Scott, unable to obtain either federal subsidies or freight to carry, had to surrender. The pattern was similar all over the western states, as financiers such as Gould were able to benefit from others' losses. But the tracks were built, and the whole nation benefited in the long run from the actions of those willing to take the risk of starting the companies. The same pattern occurred in Galveston County, where the county's investment of $500,000 was sold back to the company for $10,000. But the county and the City of Galveston did get an extremely valuable railroad as a result.[1]

Railroad building was the prime activity in the western states following the Civil War. The large cattle drives north from Texas would come and go, and agricultural production in the Great Plains would increase into the next century. But the millions of dollars invested in railroads and the excitement generated by links between the East and the Pacific Coast attracted attention. The east-west lines received most of this attention and became the legends of railroading. Sometimes lost among the Union Pacific, the Atchison, Topeka & Santa Fe, and the Southern Pacific were the north-south lines that connected Chicago and St. Louis to Texas and connected all of the western states to their seaport at Galveston. From the time in 1878 when rumors were first heard about the interest of the Southern Pacific and when the first visits in the early 1880s by former president Grant and railroad tycoons Gould and Huntington took place, Galveston was one of the focal points of western railroad activity. Denver spent a decade developing its line to Fort Worth, where it could connect first with the Gulf, Colorado & Santa Fe and then the Atchison, giving Denver access to the Gulf of Mexico.

The railroads brought multiple benefits to the state, even though many of them were not profitable. First, they provided transportation for people and goods, and helped the state gradually fill its empty space. Second, the railroads created secondary industries for materials required in their construction. The Texas & Pacific, across the state's northern tier, once ordered 500,000 crossties, and the other roads ordered according to their distances to be covered. Lumber was also required for bridges, stations, cattle pens, and cotton and freight platforms. At the peak of its construction activity the Texas & Pacific employed 8,000 laborers who laid 10,000 tons of rails and fastenings, imported from the East, but the men and teams of horses and mules required large quantities of agricultural products. Third, the construction gave rise to many construction camps along the route, which blossomed into towns such as Abilene, Eastland, Baird, Sweetwater, Colorado City, and Big Spring. Thus the railroads served as an economic stimulus to activities well beyond the track itself.[2]

Perhaps most important, the railroads created the foundation for the twentieth century. Not only were the railroads a means of transportation, they were the first large corporations in the United States and Texas, as well as Galveston.

One historian has observed that it was the Industrial Revolution and not the Civil War that divided American history into two distinct eras. The iron, steel, and railroad industries that marked the Industrial Revolution brought radical change to a way of life that had existed for two hundred years. These industries produced the first large corporations, and the railroads carried these companies into every corner of the country. The rise of regulatory bodies, such as the Texas Railroad Commission, was evidence of the power of these companies to make themselves felt throughout the economy.[3]

The railroads were among the first challenges to the budding capitalist economic system and the Wall Street markets to provide the large sums of money required for thousands of miles of track construction. On the New York Stock Exchange, 60 percent of the listed stocks were rails. When Charles H. Dow first computed an index of eleven companies in 1884, nine of those were rails.

The companies were also the first experiments in the management of large enterprises. Professional management rose in the industry after a first generation of promoters founded the companies. President J. Edgar Thompson of the Pennsylvania and Charles E. Perkins, head of the Chicago, Burlington & Quincy have been cited as two of the great managers in the East and Midwest. In the West, Jay Gould, trying to change from speculator to manager, assembled one of the best groups of executives in the country for the Missouri Pacific: General Grenville Dodge, A. L. Hopkins, A. A. Talmadge, Robert S. Hayes, and Herbert M. Hoxie. Dodge and Hoxie led the building of the Union Pacific across the Plains in the 1860s, and then came to Texas to build the Texas & Pacific for Gould. Hoxie, Talmadge, and Hayes came to Gould with the International & Great Northern, and Hopkins with the Wabash.

This was the highly experienced brainpower pool that the Gulf, Colorado & Santa Fe's George Sealy was up against during those five years he fought to maintain the independence of the GC&SF. After the purchase by the Atchison, Sealy served several years with the Boston-controlled line. He was elected chairman of the board of directors on November 12, 1888, and following that served as vice president to William B. Strong, Allen Manvel, Joseph W. Reinhart, and Aldace Walker before resigning in 1896. All of these men were at the forefront as the management and financing of the first large corporations evolved, an environment that George Sealy inhabited for almost twenty years.[4]

As one of the West's most successful independent companies before acquisition by the Atchison in a stock swap, the Gulf, Colorado & Santa Fe put its directors, stockholders, and the taxpayers of Galveston County, who originally financed it, into the thick of the railroads wars in the West. All railroad news was important news in Galveston. New construction, mergers and acquisitions, and bankruptcies could all affect Galveston's economic future, and the citizens were well aware of the potential consequences of these moves. Of course, moves of Gould and Huntington were of primary interest. When William B. Strong became president of the Atchison and aggressively began moving west, in constant conflict with Gould's Union Pacific and Missouri Pacific, his actions were closely followed. He moved to the forefront of Galveston interest, of course, when he traded stock and assumed debt in a $25,000,000 acquisition of the GC&SF in order to challenge Gould in traffic to and from Galveston. The moves of these railroad generals were compared to those of heads of armies moving their forces across the battlefields, and Galveston was not an idle bystander to these momentous events.[5]

Without the vast network of railroads feeding into Galveston, the increases in tonnage through the port would have been impossible. The *Galveston Daily News* carried advertisements from the following railroads offering service into and out of Galveston: the Southern Pacific; the Houston & Texas Central (part of the Southern Pacific); the Santa Fe; the Galveston, Houston & Henderson; the Missouri, Kansas & Texas; the Interna-

tional & Great Northern; and the Rock Island. With the Santa Fe going
to Chicago, both the Santa Fe and the Houston & Texas Central connecting with the Fort Worth & Denver City to reach Denver, and both
the Southern Pacific and the Santa Fe reaching the Pacific Coast, Galveston had rail connections into all of the major cities west of the Mississippi
River.[6]

Two dramatic events during this period were indicative of Galveston's
reaching out to the western states. On March 27, 1888, a train of the Denver, Texas & Fort Worth line arrived in Denver over the recently completed link from Fort Worth. The event completed a decade-long effort
by former governor John Evans and his Colorado associates to link Denver to the Gulf of Mexico over the tracks of the Gulf, Colorado & Santa
Fe. In August of that year Denver staged a Deep Water Convention,
chaired by Evans, to muster support throughout the West for harbor improvement at Galveston, thus linking the destinies of both cities. The
Denver convention was followed by another at Topeka in 1889. Out of this
meeting came the Interstate Deep Water committee that lobbied the Galveston appropriation through the Congress, and President Benjamin Harrison signed the bill in September, 1890.[7]

The other event that served to highlight Galveston's railroad network
as well as its shipping connections with Central and South America was
the record-setting run made in 1894 by a Santa Fe train. On March 2 a
trainload of bananas was carried from Galveston to Chicago in the record
time of 42 hours and 45 minutes, an average of 32.98 miles per hour over
the 1,410 miles. The trip was part of a Galveston campaign to expand trade
with countries to the south, but it also served to bring to the attention of
the states to the north Galveston's strategic location and the shrinking nature of the world brought about by the railroads.[8]

In the five years after deep water was achieved, Galveston exports more
than doubled from $41,886,651 to $85,657,524. Exports nearly doubled again
by 1906 to $166,857,300. Imports grew from $369,575 (a below-average
year) to $1,453,545 in 1900. By 1906 imports would be $5,018,876. Clearly
the combined impact of the deep water channel and the network of railroad connections throughout the western states rapidly had its effect upon
the city's port.[9] The construction of the Southern Pacific facilities was de-
layed by the hurricane of 1900 that devastated Galveston. But, one year
and eight months later, the docks were announced completed and ready
for business, and the port's growth resumed.[10] The increase in both exports and imports was attributed to the expanding variety of both. The su-
premacy of cotton exports was uprooted by grains, ores, minerals, cattle,
flour, and miscellaneous items. The growth of the population in the western states increased the demand for a whole range of imported items.[11]

With the dual accomplishments of deep water and extensive railroad connections, Galveston was poised to remain an important, active port until well into the next century. The transportation and exporting industries would provide an economic base of more than 10,000 jobs that would help Galveston's population grow from 37,888 in 1900 to 52,938 in 1930, and to reach a peak of 67,175 in 1960. The Gulf, Colorado & Santa Fe Railway, operating as a subsidiary of the AT&SF, maintained company headquarters in Galveston along with its depot, maintenance facilities, and yards. The Galveston Wharf Company and the Southern Pacific terminal would be thriving businesses, along with the stevedoring companies. The big cotton companies—W. L. Moody & Co., H. Kempner, and Cotton Concentration Company (owned by the Sealys)—and their offices, warehouses, and compresses enjoyed busy seasons, as did the grain elevators. Numerous steamship lines such as Lykes Brothers, the Mallory Line, Southern Pacific's Morgan Line, Waterman and Strachan made heavy use of the port and had offices. The shipping business required drydock facilities from Gray's Iron Works and Todd Shipyard, which in turn received fabrication and mechanical repair services from companies such as McDonough Iron Works, Kane's Boilerworks, and Farmer's Marine and Copper Works. Suppliers and provisioners such as Flood and Calvert and Black Hardware flourished. Numerous other freight-forwarding companies were required. Galveston was also the site of several federal agencies, including the U.S. Customs Service, the U.S. Coast Guard, and the regional headquarters of the U.S. Army Corps of Engineers, responsible for harbor maintenance, with offices and port facilities.

All of the companies mentioned were supported by a host of suppliers of goods and services, such as maritime insurance, maritime law, and construction. This vibrant economy was accomplished in spite of the technological onslaught in the twentieth century that saw superior railroad equipment, trucks and airplanes completely alter transportation in the United States.[12]

The railroad network dream envisioned in Captain Gilman's 1871 map was not fully realized. Railroads coming into Galveston from Bolivar Peninsula were not accomplished. The connections with New Orleans went though Houston. Railroads west to Mexico's Pacific Coast were also missing. However, the roads that were built covered the rest of the territory linked by the lines on Gilman's map. The names of the companies were different than those projected in 1871, but others, such as the Gulf, Colorado & Santa Fe, emerged to serve the same purposes. When one looks at a 1900 railroad map of Texas, it has the same general pattern as the Gilman map, that is, the tracks lead to the sea—at Galveston.[13]

The railroad scene at Galveston after the close of the Civil War was a tumultuous one. Some plans were never executed. Railroads that were started went bankrupt. Successful roads changed directions. Nevertheless, the results were very satisfactory to Galveston by 1900.

Caleb Forshey's planning efforts broadened Galveston horizons in the period after the war. George Sealy brought the Gulf, Colorado & Santa Fe out of bankruptcy and made it part of the vast Atchison, Topeka & Santa Fe system. Collis P. Huntington, playing a dual role, encouraged the city to achieve a deep water channel and supported the legislation in the Congress, something at which he was said to be very good, then brought in the last major railroad to feed the large terminal facilities built by the Southern Pacific. A long-range goal for Galveston set forth by the publisher of the *Galveston Daily News,* Willard Richardson, in his editorial in 1866, "Galveston and the Great West," provided the direction. In it he concluded: "If railroads are becoming important as connecting links between different points of those territories [in the West], we may well suppose that the question of railroads between those territories and their nearest seaport cannot, or should not, be long permitted to remain unagitated. We hope these suggestions as to the importance of our city, may have some tendency to promote that breadth of view upon which all important enterprise is dependent."[14]

True to Richardson's vision, the railroad links were established and, coupled with the deep water channel, enabled Galveston to become the seaport of the Great West.

It is impossible to write about Galveston and railroads without writing about the port. The port, the railroads, and the cargoes are all bound together in a single economic function and therefore mutually interdependent. Because of the incredible rate of change in the twentieth century, it has almost become a cliché to speak of "The Age of This" and "The Age of That." "The Age of the Automobile" was quickly followed by "The Age of the Airplane," then "The Nuclear Age," next "The Space Age," and now "The Age of the Internet." The world of transportation has been revolutionized by the "The Age of the Supertankers," "The Age of Containerships," and "The Age of Intermodal Transportation," the combined use of ships and rail.

The relationships between cargoes, railroads, and ports are constantly changing ones. This dizzying pace of technological progress began in the last half of the nineteenth century with electricity, the telephone, and the steamship. The increase in the size of the sailing ships forced Galveston to abandon the doctrine of natural advantage and to apply technology to the creation of a deep water port. With the coming of steam, the ships were growing even larger as the century closed.

As Houston began to plan to extend the deep water channel 50 miles up Galveston Bay and Buffalo Bayou to the outskirts of the city, it was becoming ever more obvious that people were going to reshape geography to suit their purposes. Dynamic individuals led by Tom Ball foresaw that Houston must have a deep water port to reach its goal of surpassing Galveston. Houston's civic leaders went after such a port in the early twentieth century while Galveston, reeling from the effects of the 1900 hurricane, was absorbed with its own earth-shaping projects. After suffering approximately 6,000 deaths, Galveston's attention became focused on building a seawall and raising the grade level of the low-lying barrier island. This was a time when Galveston could have been expanding its harbor facilities to make the need for Houston as a port questionable.

Both cities were very successful in their respective undertakings. Houston opened its deep water ship channel, a widened and deepened Buffalo Bayou, in 1916. Once Houston had achieved the channel and it was no longer necessary to send railroad cargoes on to Galveston, the position Houston had always held as a railroad center in the nineteenth century was fully realized. And Galveston, now sitting high and dryer, proved the success of its efforts when the city survived another severe hurricane in

1915 with relatively little damage. The city had done nothing to enhance its position as a port, while 50 miles had been cut off of the distance the railroads had to travel by reaching deep water at Houston.

With a growing population stimulated by the new petroleum industry, Houston finally began to forge ahead of the restricted Island City. This, however, did not happen overnight. It would be another fourteen years after the opening of the ship channel before Houston's total tonnage exceeded Galveston's. A comparison of exporting statistics is perhaps the best way to document the changing relationship between the two cities, and, because it is of importance at the turn of the century, cotton is the best measurement.

After Galveston achieved its 25-foot channel to the Gulf of Mexico in 1895, the city's exports doubled between 1895 and 1900. Twice during that period the city led New Orleans, when Galveston's exports passed two million bales. Shipments from Galveston began to increase after that as the Texas crop grew. Exports reached 4,046,495 bales in the 1912–13 season, and 4,036,096, in 1914–15. Galveston would have two more four-million-bale seasons even though its share of the Texas crop was declining, falling to only one million by 1940. Galveston's railroad connections with the cotton fields of Central and North Texas, of course, made these exports possible.[1]

Houston's growth as a cotton port was slow. It was 1923 before exports reach one million bales, thirty-three years after Galveston passed that mark. Houston averaged two million bales between 1925 and 1929, but after that it was Houston, not Galveston, that was challenging New Orleans to be the leading cotton port. In fact, Houston rose to third place nationally in total exports, behind New York and Los Angeles. With the rise of the oil industry in Texas and the growth of the petrochemical industries along the ship channel, King Cotton bowed to the Black Gold and became less important as an exported product.[2]

Since all of Harris County served as the tax base to support the Houston Port Authority, the port was in a position to underwrite its growth with the expansion of facilities. On the other hand, the Galveston Wharf Company struggled along as a private company until the city purchased it in 1940. Attempts were made at Galveston to expand the harbor facilities during the twentieth century, including the industrial development of neighboring Pelican Island, but these attempts were never successful. However, that is a long story in itself, and this book is already expensive enough. Let's save that for a later book.

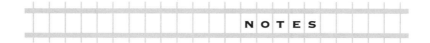
INTRODUCTION

1. Grodinsky, *Gould,* p. 398.

2. Zlatkovich, *Texas Railroads,* pp. 107–109.

3. For further information on the organization of the Missouri Pacific, see Werner, "Missouri Pacific System," pp. 777–78. For further information on the organization of the Southern Pacific, see Werner, "Southern Pacific System," pp. 1155–56.

4. Martin, *Railroads Triumphant,* p. 401.

CHAPTER 1. PLANNING EFFORTS FOR NEW RAILROADS

1. *Galveston Daily News,* July 3, 1866.

2. Ibid., July 4, 5, 1866.

3. Forshey, "Central Southern Railway," p. 279.

4. Forshey, "Atlantic and Pacific Railroad," pp. 475–83.

5. Fornell, *Galveston Era,* p. 166; McKay, "Texas and the Southern Pacific Railroads," p. 8; "Texas Railroads," pp. 523–24.

6. Forshey, "Texas Railroad System," pp. 671–76; "Texas Railroads," pp. 523–24. See Fornell, *Galveston Era,* for a complete account of Sherwood's State Plan.

7. *Galveston Daily News,* July 17, 1866.

8. Ibid., Aug. 14, 15, 1866.

9. Ibid., Aug. 22, 1866.

10. *War of the Rebellion,* pp. 214, 238.

11. Cullum, *Biographical Register,* p. 472; Hayes, *Galveston,* vol. 2, pp. 572–73; Webb, *Handbook of Texas,* vol. 2, p. 39.

12. *Galveston Daily News,* Aug. 17, 18; Sept. 5, 1866.

13. Ibid., Oct. 3, 19, 1866; Reed, *Texas Railroads,* p. 315.

14. *Galveston Daily News,* Nov. 18, 1866; Webb, *Handbook of Texas,* vol. 2, p. 57. The Central Transit was one of sixteen railroads either discussed, planned, chartered, or partially constructed during Galveston's railroad boom of the 1870s. With coast-to-coast connections, the sixteen lines running through Galveston and the sea routes indicated on a map by Captain S. H. Gilman create an impression of Galveston as the "Center of the Universe," a phrase once used to describe the city's potential. See S. H. Gilman, "The Relation of Railroads to the Commerce of Galveston," 1871, S. H. Gilman Collection. Also see the *Galveston Daily News,* June 11; July 12; Aug. 1, 1871.

15. *Galveston Daily News,* June 2; Mar. 1, 1867.

16. Reed, *Texas Railroads,* 315; *Galveston Daily News,* June 7, 8, 9, 11, 1867.

17. *Galveston Daily News,* June 14, 1867.

18. Ibid., June 16, 1867.

19. Ibid., June 20, 1867.

20. Ibid., Nov. 11, 1868.

21. Ibid., Jan. 8, 1869.

22. *Proceedings of the Southern Commercial Convention at Cincinnati,* pp. 119–22, Forshey Collection; *Galveston Daily News,* Dec. 15, 1869.

23. *Galveston Daily News,* Dec. 15, 1869.

24. "James Fredrick Joy," *Dictionary of American Biography,* vol. 10, pp. 224–25; *Railroad Gazette,* Feb. 11, 1871.

25. *Galveston Daily News,* Sept. 14, 1869.

26. Ibid., Mar. 11, 22, 1870; *Railroad Gazette,* Oct. 8, 1870.

27. *Galveston Daily News,* Mar. 31, 1870. The mining company of Phelps, Dodge & Co. was founded in 1832 when Anton G. Phelps invited his sons-in-law, William Earl Dodge and Daniel James, to join him in a partnership. The company was important in the development of copper mines at Lake Superior and iron mines in Pennsylvania. Its loans to George Scranton were important to the growth of the city of Scranton. His nephew William Walter Phelps joined the firm later. See *Dictionary of American Biography,* vol. 14, pp. 525–26.

28. *Galveston Daily News,* May 31; June 2, 1870.

29. Masterson, *Katy Railroad,* pp. 74–75; *Galveston Daily News,* July 23, 1870; Baugham, *Morgan,* pp. 196–97. The act of Congress involved here is titled "An Act granting Lands to the State of Kansas to aid in the Construction of the Kansas and Neosho Valley Railroad and its Extension to Red River [the Texas border]." Thirty-ninth Congress, Session 1, Chapter 241, 1866. Section 11 provides that either the Leavenworth, Lawrence and Fort Gibson or the Union Pacific, southern branch, in the event that one builds to the boundary of Kansas before the Neosho Valley road, may be designated by the President of the United States to build to the Red River. See George P. Sanger, ed., *The Statutes at Large, Treaties, and Proclamations of the United States of America December, 1865 to March, 1867,* vol. 14, pp. 236–39.

30. *Galveston Daily News,* Dec. 7, 1870; May 7, 10, 1872.

31. *Railroad Gazette,* Mar. 30; Apr. 13, 1872.

32. For an account of the life of Ochiltree, see Hall, "Fabulous Tom Ochiltree."

33. Baugham, *Morgan,* pp. 191–99; *Galveston Daily News,* Nov. 19; Dec. 19, 1871.

34. *Railroad Gazette,* May 25, 1872; Reed, *Texas Railroads,* pp. 375–76; Masterson, *Katy Railroad,* pp. 75–76; Baugham, *Morgan,* pp. 196–97.

35. *Railroad Gazette,* Jan. 20; Sept. 7, 1872; *New York Times,* Sept. 16, 1872; *Galveston Daily News,* July 30; Sept. 1, 1876; Werner, "Houston and Texas Central Railway," p. 742.

36. *New York Times,* July 6, 1872; Oct. 25, 1873; Reed, *Texas Railroads,* p. 319.

37. Mar. 9, 1877.

38. *Galveston Daily News,* Mar. 31, 1877.

39. *New York Times,* Mar. 16, 1877; Aug. 1, 1879; Jan. 20, 1880; Reed, *Texas Railroads,* p. 320.

40. Diary, William P. Ballinger, July 20, 1878, Rosenberg Library, Galveston.

41. *Galveston Daily News,* July 21, 1878.

42. *New York Times*, Mar. 16, 30; Apr. 6, 1877; *Galveston Daily News*, Mar. 10, 11, 12, 13, 1877.

43. *New York Times*, May 9, 13, 18, 1877; Baugham, *Morgan*, pp. 202–207; *Galveston Daily News*, May 11, 12, 13, 16, 17, 1877.

44. Baugham, *Morgan*, pp. 212–15.

CHAPTER 2. GALVESTON'S OWN RAILROAD EMERGES

1. *Galveston Daily News*, May 9, 1873.

2. Ibid. Other non-Galveston commissioners were J. P. Palmer, J. C. Higgins, W. H. Ledbetter, William K. Little, Sterling C. Robertson, J. W. Carroll, J. L. D. Morrison, Frank Latham, Thomas Allen, B. O'Connor, W. E. Scott, E. Pelot, J. S. Catlin, and W. M. Wagner.

3. Ibid., July 1, 1871; Mar. 13, 1873.

4. Ibid., June 22, 1873.

5. *New York Times*, June 21, 1873; Joseph Weidel, "Officers and Directors, Gulf Colorado and Santa Fe Railway Company," unpublished manuscripts referred to as "The Splinters," Atchison, Topeka and Santa Fe Collection, p. 2; Bradley, *Story of the Santa Fe*, pp. 9, 248; Bryant, *Atchison*, p. 127; Waters, *Steel Rails to Santa Fe*, p. 80.

6. *Galveston Daily News*, June 22, 1873. Some historians attribute the origin of the Gulf, Colorado & Santa Fe to the problems caused by the quarantine of Galveston cargoes during yellow fever epidemics and the need to bypass Houston. Quarantine does not appear to have been a significant factor, however; broader strategic goals appear to have motivated the founders.

7. Ibid., June 12, 1873; Bryant, *Atchison*, p. 127.

8. *Galveston Daily News*, June 28; July 3, 26, 1873.

9. McDonough, "Early Issues of Capital Stock," May 25, 1927, p. 3.

10. Morison and Commager, *Growth of the American Republic*, vol. 2, pp. 72–73; Tindall, *America*, pp. 700–701; Cashman, *America in the Gilded Age*, pp. 35–36; Noyes, *Thirty Years of American Finance*, pp. 17–22.

11. *Galveston Daily News*, Nov. 15, 28, 1873; Weidel, "Officers and Directors," p. 2.

12. Letters: Gen. Braxton Bragg to Col. J. P. Fresenius, Aug. 14, Sept. 18, 1874; and Gen. Braxton Bragg, "Report: Chief Engineer Bragg to the President, GC&SF Railroad Company," Oct. 29, 1874, Bragg Collection; Bryant, *Atchison*, pp. 127–29; Clark, *Then Came the Railroads*, p. 147; Bradley, *Santa Fe*, pp. 248–49; Reed, *Texas Railroads*, pp. 282–85; Carroll, *Galveston and the Gulf, Colorado and Santa Fe*, pp. 89–94; *Galveston Daily News*, Mar. 13, 1910; Mar. 13, 1917.

13. "Citizen" later turned out to be Thomas P. Ochiltree, a Republican who was elected to Congress from the Galveston District in 1880.

14. Faith, *World the Railroads Made*, pp. 89–109; Morgan, *Gilded Age*, pp. 13–30; Josephson, *Robber Barons*, pp. 222–30; Chandler, *Railroads*, pp. 48–64; Noyes, *American Finance*, pp. 62–63.

15. *Galveston Daily News*, Aug. 10, 1877.

16. Ibid., July 11; Aug. 11, 1877.

17. John Sealy was identified as one of Thomas A. Peirce's associates when he purchased the GH&H at auction in 1871 and was elected vice president of the company. Sealy resigned from the GC&SF Board of Directors April 1, 1876, when he became president of the GH&H.

18. *Galveston Daily News,* Aug. 11, 1877.

19. Ibid., Aug. 12, 1877; McDonough, "Building the Santa Fe," p. 5.

20. Letter, Gen. Braxton Bragg to Mrs. Bragg, Mar. 31, 1876, Bragg Collection.

21. *Galveston Daily News,* Aug. 14, 1877; Bryant, *Atchison,* p. 128.

22. *Galveston Daily News,* Aug. 18, 22, 1877.

CHAPTER 3. THE PATH INTO BANKRUPTCY— AND OUT

1. Galveston County Commissioners Court, Minute Book 2½, Meetings of Oct. 1, 16, 22; Dec. 5, 10, 15, 1877; McDonough, "Early Issues of Capital Stock," pp. 16–17; Weidel, "Officers and Directors," 8–9; *Galveston Daily News,* Dec. 20, 21, 1877.

2. McDonough, "Some Early History," pp. 4–5.

3. *Galveston Daily News,* Dec. 6, 1878.

4. Ibid., Dec. 10, 11, 1878.

5. Galveston County Commissioners Court, Minute Book 2½, Meeting of Dec. 13, 1878; McDonough, "Building the Santa Fe," p. 7; McDonough, "Some Early History," pp. 5–7.

6. *Galveston Daily News,* Dec. 15, 1878; McDonough, "Some Early History," pp. 5–6.

7. Galveston County Commissioners Court, Minute Book 2½, Meeting of Jan. 18, 1879.

8. Galveston County Commissioners Court, Minute Book 2½, Meeting of Mar. 14, 1879; *Galveston Daily News,* Mar. 15, 1879.

9. *Railroad Gazette,* Apr. 25, 1879; McDonough, "Building the Santa Fe," p. 8; Waters, *Steel Rails to Santa Fe,* p. 81.

10. *Railroad Gazette,* May 9, 1879; McDonough, "Building the Santa Fe," p. 8; McDonough, "Some Early History," pp. 5–9; McDonough, "Early Issues," pp. 23–27; Bryant, *Atchison,* 128; *Galveston Daily News,* Apr. 18, 1879.

11. As to the benefits to the taxpayer of the Santa Fe transaction, businessman Sampson Heidenheimer had the following to say during another Santa Fe dispute ten years later: "I am rated as the fourth largest taxpayer in the city, and I feel that the above named tax [to retire the Santa Fe bonds] has been a paying investment, and has brought in to me more benefit from the presence of the railroad and shops than many other enterprises in which I have interested myself." *Galveston Daily News,* Mar. 13, 1889.

12. McDonough, "Early Issues of Capital Stock," pp. 24–25; McDonough, "Building the Santa Fe," pp. 8–9.

13. *Railroad Gazette,* Sept. 19, 1879; McDonough, "Building the Santa Fe," p. 9; McDonough, "Early History," p. 10; *Galveston Daily News,* June 15; July 25; Oct. 1, 1879.

14. *Railroad Gazette,* Nov. 14; Oct. 17, 31, 1879; Weidel, "Officers and Directors," p. 12; McDonough, "Building the Santa Fe," p. 9; *Galveston Daily News,* Oct. 17, 26, 29; Nov. 26; Dec. 25, 27, 1879.

15. Weidel, "Officers and Directors," p. 12.

CHAPTER 4. THE RAPIDLY CHANGING WEST

1. White, *It's Your Misfortune,* pp. 243–44.

2. Ibid., p. 245.

3. Grodinsky, *Railway Strategy,* pp. 422–29; Winther, *The Transportation Frontier,* pp. 101–104; Richardson and Rister, *The Greater Southwest,* pp. 379–92; Martin, *Railroads Triumphant,* pp. 56–80.

4. *Galveston Daily News,* Sept. 18, 1874.

5. Ibid., February 13, 1878.

6. Department of the Interior, *"Abstract of the Eleventh Census: 1890,"* pp. 82–87.

7. Hayes, *Galveston,* p. 798.

8. Ibid.

9. Ibid., pp. 799–800.

10. *Galveston Daily News,* Aug. 9, 1876.

11. Ibid.

12. Ibid., Aug. 19, 1876.

13. Ibid., Aug. 19, Nov. 15, 1876.

14. Ibid., Aug. 29, 1876.

15. Ibid., Oct. 8, 1876

16. Fornell, *Galveston Era,* pp. 19–20.

17. Articles found in the Mounts, Rosenberg Library, under the headings "Galveston Wharves" and "Texas Star Flour Mills."

18. Klein, *Gould,* p. 232.

19. Ibid., p. 234.

20. *New York Times,* Nov. 15, 1879; Jan. 20, 1880; Klein, *Gould,* p. 242.

21. Klein, *Gould,* p. 243; Masterson, *Katy,* pp. 214–15.

22. Klein, *Gould,* pp. 248–50; Masterson, *Katy,* p. 215.

23. Klein, *Gould,* pp. 250–51; Grodinsky, *Railway Strategy,* pp. 166–70.

24. *New York Times,* Nov. 17, 18, 1880; Klein, *Gould,* pp. 258–59; Grodinsky, *Railway Strategy,* pp. 170–71; *Galveston Daily News,* Dec. 15, 16, 19, 20, 1880.

25. *New York Times,* Dec. 14, 1880; Klein, *Gould,* pp. 59–61; Masterson, *Katy,* pp. 217–18; *Galveston Daily News,* Dec. 16, 21, 1880.

26. Klein, *Gould,* pp. 249, 260; *New York Times,* Nov. 17, 18, 1880.

27. Klein, *Gould,* pp. 260–61.

28. *Galveston Daily News,* Mar. 24, 1880.

29. Ibid., Mar. 24, 1880; *New York Times*, Mar. 24, 1880.

30. *Galveston Daily News*, Mar. 25, 1880.

31. Ibid., Mar. 25, 1880; *New York Times*, Mar. 25, 26, 1880.

32. *New York Times*, Nov. 12, 1880; Mar. 4, 1881. Klein, *Gould*, p. 274; Grodinsky, *Strategy*, p. 168; Pletcher, *Rails*, pp. 161–62.

33. Pletcher, *Rails*, pp. 60–61; Klein, *Gould*, p. 274.

34. Pletcher, *Rails*, pp. 162–63; *Galveston Daily News*, Mar. 30, 1881.

35. *Galveston Daily News*, Mar. 8, 1881; *St. Louis Daily Globe Democrat*, Mar. 10, 16, 1881.

36. Klein, *Gould*, p. 263.

37. *Galveston Daily News*, Mar. 8, 1881.

38. Ibid.

39. Peterson, *"Jay Gould,"* p. 423; Potts, *Railroad Transportation*, p. 117; Reed, *Texas Railroads*, pp. 574–75.

40. *Galveston Daily News*, Mar. 25, 1881.

41. Ibid., Apr. 2, 1881; *New York Times*, May 7, 1880. This edition reprinted a lengthy interview with Grant from the *Chicago Inter-Ocean*, in which Grant fully presented his views on Mexico.

42. Pletcher, *Rails*, p. 163; *Railroad Gazette*, Sept. 9, 1881.

43. Pletcher, *Rails*, pp. 170–71; *New York Times*, Mar. 4, 1881.

44. *Galveston Daily News*, Feb. 3, 1881.

45. *New York Times*, Mar. 8, 1881.

46. *Galveston Daily News*, Mar. 29, 1881.

47. Pletcher, *"Consul Sutton,"* p. 373.

48. *Galveston Daily News*, Oct. 5, 1881. Reprint.

49. Ibid.

50. Pletcher, *"Consul Sutton,"* p. 391.

51. *New York Times*, Mar. 18, Apr. 18, 23, 1881; Klein, *Gould*, p. 265.

52. *Galveston Daily News*, May 22, 24, 1881.

53. Ibid., Jan. 1, 1881.

54. Ibid., May 25, 1881.

55. Klein, *Gould*, p. 270; *Railroad Gazette*, June 10, 1881; *New York Times*, June 9, 1881.

CHAPTER 5. GOULD EYES GALVESTON AND THE GC&SF

1. *Galveston Daily News*, Dec. 29, 1880. On September 28, 1880, the board of directors voted to construct a branch from Temple to Fort Worth. On September 29, 1880, the *Daily News* announced that the people of Fort Worth had subscribed to a $75,000 subsidy, assuring the decision. This turned out to be important to the company's future.

2. Ibid., Dec. 29, 1880.

3. Brockman, *Railroads, Radicals, and Democrats,* p. 232; Letter, General Grenville M. Dodge to Jay Gould, Dec. 28, 1880, Dodge Collection.

4. Letter, Dodge to Gould, Jan. 14, 1881.

5. *Galveston Daily News,* Jan. 15, 1881.

6. Ibid., Jan. 16, 1881.

7. Letter, Dodge to Gould, Jan. 20, 1881.

8. Ibid., Jan. 25, 1881.

9. Ibid., Jan. 27, 1881.

10. Gulf Colorado and Santa Fe Railway Minute Book, Atchison, Topeka and Santa Fe Collection.

11. *Galveston Daily News,* Mar. 8, 1881.

12. Ibid.

13. Ibid., Mar. 16, 1881.

14. Ibid., Mar. 29, 1881.

15. Ibid.

16. Ibid., Mar. 30, 1881.

17. Ibid., Apr. 7, 1881.

18. *Railway Gazette,* Apr. 15, 1881.

19. *Galveston Daily News,* Apr. 20, 1881.

20. Ibid., Mar. 30, 1881.

21. Ibid., Mar. 29, 1881.

22. Ibid., Apr. 28, 1881.

23. Grodinsky, *Gould,* p. 396; *Galveston Daily News,* Apr. 29, 1881; *Railway Gazette,* June 17, 1881.

24. *Galveston Daily News,* June 17, 1881.

25. Ibid., July 6, 1881. Reprint from the *St. Louis Register.*

26. *Railway Gazette,* Apr. 14; July 7, 1882.

27. *Galveston Daily News,* Jan. 13, 1882.

28. *Railway Gazette,* July 8, 1881; Grodinsky, *Gould,* p. 397.

29. *Railway Gazette,* June 2, 1882.

30. *Galveston Daily News,* May 26, 28, 1882.

31. Letter, T. J. Potter to A. E. Touzalin, May 18, 1882, Burlington Archives.

32. *Galveston Daily News,* June 7, 1882.

33. Grodinsky, *Gould,* p. 397.

34. *Railway Gazette,* May 26, 1882.

35. *Galveston Daily News,* May 28, 1882.

36. Ibid., May 30; July 16, 1882.

37. *Railway Gazette,* Aug. 11, 1882.

38. *Galveston Daily News,* July 18, 1882.

39. Grodinsky, *Gould,* p. 397.

40. *Galveston Daily News,* Dec. 10, 1882.

41. Grodinsky, *Gould,* p. 397.

42. *Galveston Daily News,* Oct. 21, 1882.

43. Ibid., Dec. 29, 1882.

44. Ibid., Mar. 27, 1883.

45. Ibid., Apr. 1, 1883.

46. Ibid., May 3, 4, 1883.

47. Ibid., May 4, 5, 1883.

48. Ibid., May 5, 1883.

49. *New York Times*, Mar. 3; Apr. 5, 22, 1883.

50. Ibid., May 15, 1883.

51. "Agreement to Hold Stock," Gulf, Colorado and Santa Fe Collection. Although the agreement was revealed in 1883, it had actually been executed January 24, 1881, and signed by twenty-three major stockholders. *Galveston Daily News*, June 10, 17, 1883.

52. GC&SF Minute Book, Aug. 1, 1883; Grodinsky, *Gould,* p. 398.

53. *Galveston Daily News,* Dec. 1, 1883; *New York Times,* Dec. 2, 1883.

54. *Galveston Daily News,* Oct. 18; Nov. 15, 1883.

55. *Railroad Gazette,* Aug. 8, 1884.

56. *Galveston Daily News,* Aug. 8, 9, 1884.

57. Ibid., Jan. 2, 24; Feb. 28, 1884.

58. Ibid., Mar. 5, 30; Apr. 7, 1884.

59. Foreman, *Oklahoma,* pp. 173–75, 178; Harlow, *Oklahoma,* pp. 224–25.

60. Foreman, *Oklahoma,* pp. 216, 239–40; Harlow, *Oklahoma,* pp. 240–42.

61. Foreman, *Oklahoma,* pp. 201, 227.

62. Ibid., p. 230; Harlow, *Oklahoma,* pp. 249, 260–61; Littlefield, *Cherokee Freedmen,* pp. 38–39.

63. *Railroad Gazette,* Aug. 1, 1884.

64. *Galveston Daily News,* Apr. 7, 1884. The Supreme Court case cited here is the *United States, Use of James Mackey et al., Plaintiffs in Error v. Richard S. Cox, 18 Howard 100–106.* The case can be found in Stephen K. Williams, ed., *Cases Argued and Decided in the Supreme Court of the United States, Book 15, Lawyers Edition, 18 Howard, 100–106.* 1960 reprint, pp. 299–302. Benjamin C. Howard was the Reporter for the Decisions of the Supreme Court. The cases he reported are contained in twenty-four volumes. In the reprint, volumes 17, 18, 19, and 20 are contained in Book 15. The Books of the reprint use dual page numbers.

65. Ibid., Apr. 7, 1884.

66. *Galveston Daily News,* June 2, 20, 22; July 1, 1884.

67. Ibid., July 5, 6, 1884.

68. Ibid., July 6, 1884.

69. Ibid.

70. Ibid.

71. McDonough, "Building the Santa Fe," p. 27.

72. *Railroad Gazette,* Oct. 31, 1884; McDonough, "Building the Santa Fe," p. 27.

73. *Galveston Daily News,* Oct. 10, 14; Nov. 2, 1884; *Railroad Gazette,* Nov. 7, 1884.

74. *Railroad Gazette,* Nov. 7, 1884.

75. *Galveston Daily News,* Nov. 2, 1884.

Chapter 6. Gould Stymied: First the Pool, Then the Sale

1. Gulf, Colorado and Santa Fe Railway Minute Book, Mar. 3, 1885, p. 303.
2. Ibid., p. 304.
3. *Galveston Daily News,* Apr. 6, 1885.
4. Letter, Alexander C. Hutchinson to Collis P. Huntington, June 28, 1885, Huntington Collection. Correspondents hereafter referred to as ACH and CPH. After Huntington acquired the Morgan interests, he renamed it Southern Pacific Eastern Division and made Hutchinson, who had been with Morgan, president.
5. Letter, CPH to George Sealy, July 2, 1885, Huntington Collection.
6. Gulf, Colorado and Santa Fe Minute Book, July 13, 1885, p. 341.
7. *Galveston Daily News,* July 9, 1885; *Railway Gazette,* July 3, 1885.
8. Letter, ACH to CPH, July 4, 1885, Huntington Collection.
9. Letter, CPH to ACH, July 11, 1885, Huntington Collection.
10. Letter, ACH to CPH, July 11, 1885, Huntington Collection.
11. *Galveston Daily News,* July 16, 1885.
12. Reed, *Texas Railroads,* pp. 552–53.
13. Letter, CPH to ACH, July 17, 1885, Huntington Collection.
14. Ibid.
15. Letter, ACH to CPH, July 20, 1885, Huntington Collection.
16. Letter, ACH to CPH, July 21, 1885, Huntington Collection.
17. Letter, ACH to CPH, July 23, 1885, Huntington Collection.
18. *Galveston Daily News,* July 24, 1885; *Railway Gazette,* July 31, 1885, p. 493.
19. Letter, ACH to CPH, July 27, 1885, Huntington Collection.
20. Letter, H. M. Hoxie to A. L. Hopkins, July 25, 1885, Huntington Collection.
21. Letter, CPH to ACH, Aug. 4, 1885, Huntington Collection.
22. *Galveston Daily News,* Aug. 5, 1885.
23. Gulf, Colorado and Santa Fe Minute Book, Aug. 3, 1885; *Railway Gazette,* Aug. 7, 1885, p. 509.
24. *Galveston Daily News,* Aug. 5, 1885.
25. Ibid., Aug. 6, 1885.
26. Letter, ACH to CPH, Aug. 5, 1885, Huntington Collection.
27. Ibid., Aug. 6, 1885.
28. Ibid.
29. *New York Times,* Aug. 13, 1885.
30. Gulf, Colorado and Santa Fe Minute Book, Aug. 12, 1885, p. 343.
31. *New York Times,* Aug. 14, 1885; *Galveston Daily News,* Aug. 14, 1885.
32. Letter, ACH to CPH, Aug. 14, 1885, Huntington Collection; *Galveston Daily News,* Aug. 15, 1885.
33. Letter, ACH to CPH, Aug. 13, 1885, Huntington Collection.
34. Letter, CPH to ACH, Aug. 17, 1885, Huntington Collection.
35. *Railway Gazette,* Aug. 28, 1885, p. 557.

36. Gulf Colorado and Santa Fe Minute Book, Aug. 24, 1885, p. 353, and Sept. 5, 1885, p. 354; Reed, *Texas Railroads,* p. 553.

37. *Galveston Daily News,* Sept. 6, 1885; Reed, *Texas Railroads,* p. 553.

38. Letter, ACH to CPH, Sept. 8, 1885, Huntington Collection.

39. Ibid.

40. Circular No. 1, Texas Traffic Association, Sept. 4, 1885, Huntington Collection; *Railway Gazette,* Sept. 24, 1885, p. 622.

41. *Galveston Daily News,* Oct. 17, 1885.

42. Letter, ACH to CPH, Oct. 18, 1885, Huntington Collection.

43. Letter, Herbert M. Hoxie to A. L. Hopkins, Nov. 10, 1885, Huntington Collection.

44. Although the pool may have accomplished immediate goals for President Sealy, the agreement was to have a short life. True to his campaign promises, Attorney General James S. Hogg filed suit in the Travis County (Austin) District Court, charging the pool with violating Article X, Section 5 of the Texas Constitution. In April, 1888, Judge John C. Townes granted a permanent injunction against the members of the pool. The pool appealed the decision of the Texas Supreme Court, which upheld the decision of the lower court on December 21, 1888. For further details, see Cotner, *Hogg,* 154–57, and Spratt, *Road to Spindletop,* 34–36.

45. *Galveston Daily News,* Aug. 30, 31; Sept. 1, 2, 3, 1885; *New York Times,* Aug. 28, 30, 31; Sept. 1, 4, 1885; *Railway Gazette,* Sept. 4, 11, 1885.

46. Letter, George Sealy to William B. Strong, Dec. 4, 1885, Gulf, Colorado and Santa Fe Collection.

47. Pinckard and Pinckard, *Lest We Forget,* p. D-1.

48. Letter, Strong to Sealy, Feb. 9, 1886, Gulf, Colorado and Santa Fe Collection.

49. Ibid.

50. Contract between the Atchison, Topeka and Santa Fe Railroad Co. and the Gulf, Colorado and Santa Fe Railway Co., Mar. 3, 1886, Atchison, Topeka and Santa Fe Collection, Kansas State Historical Society, Topeka.

51. Ibid.

52. Ratification of the Contract of Mar. 3, 1886, with the Atchison, Topeka and Santa Fe Railroad Co. by the GC&SF Directors, Gulf, Colorado and Santa Fe Collection.

53. Amendment to the Contract of Mar. 3, 1886, signed Mar. 30, 1886, Gulf, Colorado and Santa Fe Collection. Historian Keith L. Bryant Jr. offers the most straightforward explanation of the transaction: "The contract signed on March 3, 1886, by Strong and Sealy called for the transfer of the entire capital stock to the GC&SF to the Atchison in exchange for $8 million in Atchison stock. The Santa Fe [Atchison] also assumed the $12,000 per mile in first-mortgage bonds and $5,000 per mile in second-mortgage bonds of the GC&SF for a total security exchange of $25,000 per mile (or $25,000,000 for the 1,000 miles). On March 23, the stockholders of the GC&SF elected representatives of the Atchison to their board, and the next year on March 8, the officers of the Atchison became the officers of the GC&SF, thus completing the merger." Bryant, *Atchison,* p. 133.

54. Spence, *Jones,* pp. 48–49; Sherman, "Early Days."

55. Spence *Jones*, p. 49; Bryant, *Atchison*, p. 133.

56. Spence, *Jones*, pp. 49–50; Reed, *Texas Railroads*, pp. 290–91.

57. Letter, Strong to Sealy, Nov. 15, 1886, Gulf Colorado and Santa Fe Collection.

58. "Directors and Officers," Atchison, Topeka and Santa Fe Railroad Company, Jan. 1, 1887, Atchison, Topeka and Santa Fe Collection, Baker Library, Harvard Graduate School of Business Administration, Boston.

59. Fifteenth Annual Report of the Board of Directors, Atchison, Topeka and Santa Fe Railroad Company, Dec. 31, 1886, Atchison, Topeka and Santa Fe Collection, Baker Library, p. 23.

60. Weidel, "Officers and Directors," Atchison, Topeka and Santa Fe Collection, p. 19.

61. *Galveston Daily News*, May 13, 14, and 15, 1887.

62. Ibid., May 15, 1887.

63. Ibid., May 25, 1887. Historian George C. Werner states that the St. Louis & Chicago purchase was not completed, although the *Galveston Daily News* reported that all of the executives were together for the final step of the negotiations.

64. Ibid., June 5, 1887.

65. Ibid., June 15, 1887.

66. The agreement may not have been as significant to the Mallory line as it was to Galveston, since the Mallorys had similar agreements with the Gould lines at the time. Starting in 1870 with the agreement with the Galveston, Houston & Henderson railroad, the Mallory lines benefited as Gould's Missouri Pacific took over the MKT, the I&GN, and the GH&H. Baugham, *Mallorys of Mystic*, 179–81.

67. *Galveston Daily News*, May 18, 1887.

68. Ibid.

69. Ibid., June 5, 1887.

70. Grodinsky, *Transcontinental Railway Strategy*, pp. 215, 223, 301–303; Klein, *Gould*, pp. 414–21, 441–44; Reigel, "Missouri Pacific," pp. 190–96. For further information on the MKT, see Hofsommer, "Missouri-Kansas-Texas Railroad," pp. 776–77. For further information on the I&GN, see Werner, "International-Great Northern Railroad," pp. 861–62.

CHAPTER 7. HUNTINGTON LOOKS EASTWARD

1. Yenne, *Southern Pacific*, pp. 23, 31, 42, 51. Huntington's interest in Galveston is reflected in this significant entry Judge William P. Ballinger made in his diary on June 10, 1879: "Long interview with [John H.] Hutchings tonight. Says [George] Flournoy brings back most attractive accounts of prospects of Huntington's road [Southern Pacific] terminating at Galveston. This would give us a boom higher than a tidal wave." Judge William P. Ballinger Diary.

2. *Railroad Gazette*, June 24; July 22, 1881. Hofsommer, *Southern Pacific*. Although the title of this book indicates it covers the years 1901–1985, it does contain the history of events leading up to 1901. This book is especially good on matters of corporate organization.

3. *Railroad Gazette,* Oct. 21, 1881; Hofsommer, *Southern Pacific,* p. 7.

4. *Railroad Gazette,* Oct. 21, 1881.

5. Ibid., Nov. 22; Dec. 2, 1881; Hofsommer, *Southern Pacific,* p. 161.

6. O'Connor, *Gould's Millions,* pp. 224–26; Klein, *Gould,* pp. 270–71.

7. *New York Times,* Nov. 17, 1881; *Railroad Gazette,* Nov. 18; Dec. 2, 1881; Yenne, *Southern Pacific,* p. 51; Klein, *Gould,* pp. 270–71; Hofsommer, *Southern Pacific,* p. 161.

8. *Galveston Daily News,* Dec. 2, 9, 13, 1881; Hofsommer, *Southern Pacific,* p. 161.

9. *Galveston Daily News,* Jan. 27, 1882; Klein, *Gould,* p. 271.

10. *Galveston Daily News,* Feb. 1, 3, 4, 18, 1882; Klein, *Gould,* p. 271.

11. *Galveston Daily News,* Feb. 23, 1882; Hofsommer, *Southern Pacific,* p. 163.

12. *Galveston Daily News,* Mar. 22, 1882.

13. Ibid., July 28, 1882.

14. Ibid., Aug. 5; Dec. 10, 1882.

15. Ibid., Nov. 3, 1882.

16. Yenne, *Southern Pacific,* p. 51; Klein, *Gould,* pp. 304–305; *Galveston Daily News,* Feb. 25; May 5; June 3, 1883; Hofsommer, *Southern Pacific,* pp. 159–63.

17. *Galveston Daily News,* Sept. 2; Oct. 1, 13, 1883.

18. Ibid., Mar. 11, 1884.

19. Ibid., Sept. 26, 1884.

20. Wilson and Taylor, *Southern Pacific,* pp. 102–103; Hofsommer, *Southern Pacific,* p. 5. The Southern Pacific System, also known as the Sunset Route, from San Francisco to New Orleans was composed of several companies: Southern Pacific of California, Southern Pacific of Arizona, Southern Pacific of New Mexico, the Galveston, Harrisburgh & San Antonio, and the Texas & New Orleans. The GH&SA and T&NO comprised the Atlantic system; the others were in the Pacific system. The Louisville, New Orleans & Texas, extending from New Orleans to Newport News, Virginia, was a Huntington road but not part of the Southern Pacific System.

CHAPTER 8. THE SOUTHERN PACIFIC COMES TO GALVESTON

1. *Galveston Daily News,* May 12, 13, 1896.

2. Ibid.

3. Ibid., Mar. 16, 1896.

4. Ibid., Mar. 27, 1898.

5. Letter, Collis P. Huntington to George Sealy, Mar. 31, 1898, Galveston City Company Records.

6. Ibid.

7. Letter, E. A. Hawkins to John H. Hutchings, president of the Galveston City Company, June 11, 1898, Galveston City Company Records.

8. *Galveston Tribune,* Aug. 19, 1898.

9. *Galveston Daily News,* July 28, 1882.

10. Agreements with William J. Jones, et al., Huntington Collection.

11. Ibid.
12. *Galveston Daily News,* Oct. 1, 7, 13, 1883; Sept. 26, 1884.
13. Ibid., Mar. 3, 20, 1885.
14. *Galveston Tribune,* Oct. 10, 15, 20, 22, 1898.
15. Letter, Huntington to Hawkins, Nov. 17, 1898; Hawkins to John H. Hutchings, Nov. 29, 1898, Galveston City Company Records.
16. Letter, Hawkins to Hutchings, Dec. 8, 1898; Hawkins to Hutchings, Dec. 10, 1898; Hawkins to Hutchings, Dec. 14, 1898; Hawkins to Huntington, Dec. 15, 1898, Galveston City Company Records.
17. *Galveston Daily News,* Jan. 1; Mar. 29, 1899.
18. *Galveston Tribune,* July 19; Dec. 11, 1897.
19. *Galveston Tribune,* Oct. 8, 1898.
20. *Galveston Tribune,* Jan. 19, 1898; *Galveston Daily News,* Jan. 31; Mar. 29, 1899.
21. *Galveston Tribune,* Feb. 3, 6; Mar. 29; May 1, 5, 1899.
22. *Galveston Daily News,* Mar. 16, 1900; Wilson and Taylor, *Southern Pacific,* p. 106.
23. *Galveston Daily News,* Mar. 16, 1900; The *News* identified the train as the Houston East & West Texas. In his first interview, Huntington was asked if the purchase of the HE&WT was complete yet. He answered that it was almost completed and that he expected a telegram within the next two days announcing the closing of the matter. The HE&WT retained its identity until it was incorporated into the Texas & New Orleans.
24. Ibid., Mar. 17, 1900. Following Huntington's death in August, 1900, the Panama Canal was built and eventually had a large effect upon the profitability of the railroad. See Reed, *Texas Railroads,* p. 254.
25. *Galveston Daily News,* Mar. 17, 1900.
26. Ibid.
27. Ibid.
28. Ibid., Mar. 18, 1900. The Southern Pacific System bought the Galveston, Houston & Northern in 1905, giving the Southern Pacific its own tracks and bridge into Galveston, and merged the GH&N with the Galveston, Harrisburg & San Antonio. See Reed, *Texas Railroads,* pp. 252–53.
The Southern Pacific would provide continuous passenger service between Galveston and Houston for 46 years before stopping the daily runs in 1951. See Young, "SP's 172."

CONCLUSION

1. Grodinsky, *Transcontinental Railway Strategy,* pp. 422–25.
2. Spratt, *Spindletop,* p. 33.
3. Klein, *Gould,* pp. 491–92; Spratt, *Spindletop,* pp. 34–36; Faith, *World the Railroads Made,* pp. 213–17.
4. Weidel, "Officers of the Santa Fe," pp. 21–28; Klein, *Gould,* p. 263; Missouri Pacific Railway, Annual Report, 1882; Martin, *Railroads Triumphant,* pp. 260, 298;

Lowenstein, "Charles Dow's Vision." The first Dow Jones Industrial Average was published May 26, 1896. It included twelve stocks, of which General Electric is the lone survivor.

5. Faith, *World the Railroads Made*, pp. 210–13.

6. The Galveston, Houston & Henderson Railroad was jointly owned by the MKT and the I&GN, and both used the GH&H tracks. Although the Rock Island advertised in Galveston, it must have been necessary to connect with it in Fort Worth or Dallas.

7. Young, *Galveston and the Great West*, pp. 114–49.

8. Ibid., pp. 184–85.

9. "Port of Galveston."

10. "Southern Pacific System."

11. *Galveston Daily News*, Sept. 1, 1900.

12. Interviews with John Unbehagen, Mayor of Galveston, 1977–78, and former owner of Flood and Calvert. Population numbers are from the Texas Almanac. Martin, *Railroads Triumphant*, pp. 359–75. Writing near the end of the twentieth century, Martin, in his final chapter, "Enterprise Triumphant," views railroads as having a rebirth and projects their role into the twenty-first century.

13. Zlatkovich, *Texas Railroads*, p. 111.

14. *Galveston Daily News*, May 3, 1866.

EPILOGUE

1. *Galveston Daily News*, Apr. 11, 1942. This centennial edition contained a chart showing the Texas cotton crop and cotton receipts at Galveston from 1865 to 1940. The edition contained much information of interest to historians.

2. Sibley, *Port of Houston*, pp. 132, 155, 161, 168–69.

PUBLISHED SOURCES

Baugham, James P. *Charles Morgan and the Development of Southern Transportation.* Nashville: Vanderbilt University Press, 1968.

———. *The Mallorys of Mystic.* Middletown, Conn.: Published for Maritime Historical Association by Wesleyan University Press, 1972.

Bradley, Glenn. D. *The Story of the Santa Fe.* Boston: Gorham, 1920.

Brockman, John Martin. "Railroads, Radicals, and Democrats: A Study in Texas Politics." Ph.D. diss., University of Texas, 1975.

Bryant, Keith L., Jr. *History of the Atchison, Topeka and Santa Fe Railway.* New York: Macmillan, 1974.

Carroll, John M. *Galveston and the Gulf, Colorado and Santa Fe Railroad.* Galveston: Center for Transportation and Commerce, 1985.

Cashman, Sean Dennis. *America in the Gilded Age.* New York: New York University Press, 1988.

Chandler, Alfred D., Jr. *The Railroads: The Nation's First Big Business.* New York: Ayer, 1981.

Clark, Ira G. *Then Came the Railroads.* Norman: University of Oklahoma Press, 1958.

Cotner, James. C. *James Stephen Hogg.* Austin: University of Texas Press, 1959.

Cullum, George W. *Biographical Register of Officers and Graduates of the U.S. Military Academy at West Point,* vol. 1. Boston: Houghton Mifflin, 1891.

Dictionary of American Biography. New York: Scribner's Sons, 1933.

Faith, Nicholas. *The World the Railroads Made.* New York: Carroll and Graf, 1990.

Foreman, Grant. *A History of Oklahoma.* Norman: University of Oklahoma Press, 1952.

Fornell, Earl Wesley. *The Galveston Era: The Texas Crescent on the Eve of Secession.* Austin: University of Texas Press, 1961.

Forshey, Caleb. G. "Atlantic and Pacific Railroad." *Commercial Review of the South and West* 3 (1847): 475–83.

———. "Central Southern Railway." *Commercial Review of the South and West* 1 (1846): 279.

———. "Texas Railroad System." *DeBow's Southern and Western Review* 18 (1855): 671–76.

Garrett, Julia Kathryn. *Fort Worth: A Frontier Triumph.* Austin: Encino, 1972.

Grodinsky, Julius. *Jay Gould, His Business Career, 1867–1892.* Philadelphia: University of Pennsylvania Press, 1957.

———. *Transcontinental Railway Strategy, 1869–1893: A Study of Businessmen.* Philadelphia: University of Pennsylvania Press, 1962.

Hall, Claude H. "The Fabulous Tom Ochiltree: Promoter, Politician, and Raconteur," *Southwestern Historical Quarterly* 71, no. 3 (1968): 347–76.

Harlow, Victor E. *Oklahoma: Its Origin and Development.* Oklahoma City: Harlow, 1950.

Hayes, Charles W. *Galveston: A History of the Island and the City.* Austin: Jenkins Garrett, 1974.

Hofsommer, Donovan L. "Missouri-Kansas-Texas Railroad." In *The New Handbook of Texas,* edited by Ron Tyler, vol. 4, pp. 776–77. Austin: Texas State Historical Association, 1996.

————. *Southern Pacific, 1901–1985.* College Station: Texas A&M University Press, 1986.

Huxtable, Nils. *Classic North American Steam.* New York: Smithmark Publishers, Inc., 1993.

Josephson, Matthew. *The Robber Barons.* New York: Harcourt, Brace, 1962.

Klein, Maury. *The Legend of Jay Gould.* Baltimore: Johns Hopkins University Press, 1986.

Larson, John Lauritz. *Bonds of Enterprise: John Murray Forbes and Western Development in America's Railway Age.* Boston: Division of Research, Graduate School of Business Administration, Harvard University, 1984. Distributed by Harvard University Press.

Littlefield, Daniel F. *The Cherokee Freedmen.* Westport, Conn.: Greenwood, 1978.

Lowenstein, Roger. "Charles Dow's Vision Was Well Above the Average." *Wall Street Journal,* Jan. 8, 1996.

McComb, David G. *Galveston: A History.* Austin: University of Texas Press, 1986.

McKay, S. S. "Texas and the Southern Pacific Railroad." *Southwestern Historical Quarterly* 35, no. 1 (1931): 7–15.

Martin, Albro. *Railroads Triumphant.* Oxford: Oxford University Press, 1992.

Masterson, V. V. *The Katy Railroad and the Last Frontier.* Norman: University of Oklahoma Press, 1952.

Morgan, H. Wayne, ed. *The Gilded Age.* 1963. Rpt., Syracuse: Syracuse University Press, 1970.

Morison, Samuel Eliot, and Henry Steele Commager. *The Growth of the American Republic.* New York: Oxford University Press, 1962.

Noyes, Alexander Dana. *Thirty Years of American Finance.* 1900. Rpt., New York: Greenwood, 1969.

O'Connor, Richard. *Gould's Millions.* Westport, Conn.: Greenwood, 1962.

Peterson, Robert L. "Jay Gould and the Railroad Commission of Texas." *Southwestern Historical Quarterly* 58, no. 4 (1955): 422–32.

Pinckard, Jane Burton, and Rebecca Sealy Pinckard. *Lest We Forget: The Open Gates.* Houston: Published by the Authors, 1988. (Copy in Rosenberg Library, Galveston.)

Pletcher, David M. "Consul Warren P. Sutton and American-Mexican Border Trade during the Early Diaz Period." *Southwestern Historical Quarterly* 79, no. 4 (1976): 373–99.

————. *Rails, Mines, and Progress: Seven American Promoters in Mexico, 1867–1911.* Ithaca: Cornell University Press, 1958.

Potts, Charles S. *Railroad Transportation in Texas.* Austin: University of Texas Press, 1909.

Rapp, William F. "The Galveston, Houston and Henderson Railroad." *Railway History Monograph* 15, nos. 2, 3, 4 (1986).

Reed, St. Clair G. *A History of Texas Railroads.* Houston: St. Clair Publishing, 1941.

Reigel, R. E. "The Missouri Pacific, 1879–1900," *Missouri Historical Review* 28 (1924): 190–96.

Richardson, Rupert Norval, and Carl Coke Rister. *The Greater Southwest.* Glendale, Calif.: Arthur H. Clark, 1935.

Sanger, George P. *The Statutes at Large, Treaties, and Proclamations of the United States of America, December 1865 to March 1867.* Vol. 14. Boston: Little, Brown and Company, 1868.

Sherman, Walter Justin. "Early Days on the Texas Santa Fe," *Historical Society of Northwestern Ohio, Quarterly Bulletin* 6, no. 4 (1934).

Sherwood, Lorenzo. *Proposed National System of Cheap Freight Railways.* Washington, D.C.: National Cheap Freight Railway League, 1867.

Sibley, Marilyn McAdams. *The Port of Houston; A History.* Austin: University of Texas Press, 1968.

Spence, Vernon G. *Colonel Morgan Jones.* Norman: University of Oklahoma Press, 1971.

Spratt, John Stricklin. *The Road to Spindletop: Economic Change in Texas, 1875–1901.* Austin: University of Texas Press, 1988.

Taliaferro, Henry G., Jane Kenamore, and Uri Haller. *Cartographic Resources in the Rosenberg Library.* College Station: Texas A&M University Press, 1988.

Taylor, Virginia. *The Franco-Texan Land Company.* Austin: University of Texas Press, 1969.

"Texas Railroads." *DeBow's Southern and Western Review* 1, no. 5 (Nov. 1852), pp. 523–25.

Tindall, George Brown. *America: A Narrative History.* New York: Norton, 1984.

Waters, L. L. *Steel Rails to Santa Fe.* Lawrence: University of Kansas Press, 1950.

Webb, Walter Prescott, ed. *The Handbook of Texas.* Austin: Texas State Historical Association, 1952.

Werner, George C. "Houston and Texas Central Railway." In *The New Handbook of Texas,* edited by Ron Tyler, vol. 3, p. 742. Austin: Texas State Historical Association, 1996.

———. "International-Great Northern Railroad." In *The New Handbook of Texas,* edited by Ron Tyler, vol. 3, pp. 861–62. Austin: Texas State Historical Association, 1996.

———. "Missouri Pacific System." In *The New Handbook of Texas,* edited by Ron Tyler, vol. 4, pp. 777–78. Austin: Texas State Historical Association, 1996.

———. "Southern Pacific System." In *The New Handbook of Texas,* edited by Ron Tyler, vol. 5, pp. 1155–56. Austin: Texas State Historical Association, 1996.

White, Richard. *It's Your Misfortune and None of My Own: A History of the American West.* Norman: University of Oklahoma Press, 1991.

Williams, Stephen K. *Cases Argued and Decided in the Supreme Court of the United States, Book 15, Lawyers Edition.* Reprint, Rochester, N.Y.: The Lawyers Cooperative Publishing Co., 1960.

Wilson, Neill C., and Frank J. Taylor. *Southern Pacific: The Roaring Story of a Fighting Railroad.* New York: McGraw-Hill, 1952.

Winther, Oscar O. *The Transportation Frontier: Trans-Mississippi West, 1865–1890.* New York: Holt, Rinehart and Winston, 1964.

Yenne, Bill. *Southern Pacific.* New York: Bonanza, 1985.

Young, Earle B. *Galveston and the Great West.* College Station: Texas A&M University Press, 1997.

———. "SP's 172 to Make Last Run to Houston Saturday," *Galveston Tribune,* Aug. 3, 1951.

Zlatkovich, Charles. *Texas Railroads: A Record of Construction and Abandonment.* Austin: Bureau of Business Research, University of Texas, and Texas State Historical Association, 1981.

UNPUBLISHED DOCUMENTS

Atchison, Topeka and Santa Fe Collection, Baker Library, Harvard Graduate School of Business Administration, Boston.

Ballinger, Judge William P., Diary, Rosenberg Library, Galveston.

Bragg, Gen. Braxton, Collection, Rosenberg Library, Galveston.

Burlington Archives, Newberry Library, Chicago.

Dodge, Gen. Grenville M., Collection, State Historical Society of Iowa, Des Moines.

Forshey, Caleb G., Collection, Rosenberg Library, Galveston.

Galveston City Company Records, Rosenberg Library, Galveston.

Gilman, S. H., Collection, Rosenberg Library, Galveston.

Gulf, Colorado and Santa Fe Collection, Rosenberg Library, Galveston.

Gulf, Colorado and Santa Fe Railway Minute Book, Atchison, Topeka and Santa Fe Collection, Kansas State Historical Collection, Topeka.

Huntington, Collis P., Collection, Library of Congress, Washington, D.C.

Kopperl, Moritz, Scrapbook, Rosenberg Library, Galveston.

McDonough, Elinore, Unpublished Manuscripts, Atchison, Topeka and Santa Fe Collection, Kansas State Historical Society, Topeka.

Missouri Pacific Railway, Annual Report, 1882, Missouri Pacific Collection, St. Louis Public Library, St. Louis.

"The Port of Galveston," Galveston Commercial Association, October, 1918, Galveston Wharves Collection, Rosenberg Library, Galveston.

"The Southern Pacific System," May, 1901, Southern Pacific Collection, Rosenberg Library, Galveston.

Texas Traffic Association, Circular No. 1. Huntington Collection, Library of Congress, Washington, D.C.

Weidel, Joseph, Unpublished Manuscripts, Atchison, Topeka and Santa Fe Collection, Kansas State Historical Society, Topeka.

GOVERNMENT DOCUMENTS

Department of the Interior. *Abstract of the Eleventh Census: 1890.* Washington, D.C.: Government Printing Office, 1894.

Galveston County Commissioners Court Minute Book 2$^1/_2$, County Court House, Galveston.

United States Supreme Court, 1870–1871, No. 212, *Tucker, et al. vs. Cowdrey, Galveston, Houston and Henderson Railroad, et al.*

The War of the Rebellion: A Compilation of the Official Records of the Union and Confederate Armies, series 1, vol. 15. Washington, D.C.: Government Printing Office, 1880.